Cathedral

of

Angels

How to obtain a profound connection with the Angelic
Realms that will change your life forever

Cover Design by www.errolgee.com

Edited by Amanda Sweeney, Marcus Soyke-Matthews and Chad Manian

www.LidiaFrederico.com

Contents

Introduction

Many books have been written about angels. If you have read any of them, I would like to suggest that this book will take you to the next level. It can also be read in its own right. On reading this book you will touch the core of the angelic realms by learning how to use angels to assist you in every area of your life.

Working with angels is the most magnificent experience a human being can have. The magnitude of these experiences is beyond what words can express, you just have to open your heart and feel it. To do this there is first a process of understanding and learning then putting the knowledge into practice. Just like any workout, practice makes perfect, and your angels will be with you along your new amazing journey.

To start with, all you need to do is open your heart wide and invite the angelic realms into your life, and then watch miracles occur day after day.

In this book you will learn how to deeply connect with your guardian angel and with the angelic realms, creating a bond for life. I can tell you it's the most extraordinary experience you will ever have in your life!

All the information in this book has been channelled by my Ascended Masters. It has given me great joy to write it as I love to work with angels and I'm sure that you will too.

The Angelic Realm

Part 1

CHAPTER ONE

What is an Angel?

The word "Angel" is thought to derive from the Greek word "angelos" which means 'messenger'. In Christian, Muslim, Jewish and other theologies, an angel can be one who acts as a messenger, attendant or agent of God/Goddess/Universe.

Angels are the true Messengers of the essence of God/ Universe. The messages they are asked to carry and transmit to us is beyond human experience and include words, light, energy, vibration, colour, emotion/feelings, fragrances and even thoughts. The messages sent by these pure angelic beings are multi-dimensional; every single angelic message is infused with the most pure divine essence, a direct message, a powerful and loving expression of God.

Angels have never existed in human form, nor do humans become angels when they cross over, it is important to understand this. The angels tune into the energetic frequencies of humans so we are able to sense, feel, hear, see and even smell their perfume when they are present. I've taught many people how to invoke Angels, and many come back to me saying that they smelled the pure scent of flowers like jasmine, roses, lilacs, or violets after invoking angels. An awe-inspiring experience, is all I can say! As you learn how to connect with your angels, they will teach and guide you on how to sense them with one of your five senses, and the wonder is that you will then find your "true sixth sense".

Angels are the essence of pure unconditional love and joy, they stem from the heart of God/Universe.

Angels are a bridge, a pathway between the physical realm and the spiritual realm, allowing us access to their pure spiritual energy that embodies God's perfect and unconditional love for us. They bring heaven to earth and create doorways you can step through to awaken the divine essence within.

There are many different kinds of Angels and they are assigned different types of "jobs". Each Angel serves a different function in your life. For instance, there are Archangels, Messenger Angels, Seraphims, Guardian Angels and many more that I will discuss later in the book. In times of great need, Messenger Angels can take on human form for short periods of time to give you a message or help you with something important in your life or others around you. A Guardian Angel is an assistant, guide and personal protector. Every single one of us has a Guardian Angel, whether you want it or not; as they are assigned to us by God to always look over us, from before your birth and beyond the time you cross over.

CHAPTER TWO

The Angelic Hierarchy

The Angelic Realm has a hierarchy, just like the army. Depending on its level in the hierarchy, an angel will have different honours and duties.

There are nine distinct orders of angels which in turn fall under three major headings known as choirs.

First Choir	Second Choir	Third Choir
Seraphim	Dominations	Principalities
Cherubim	Virtues	Archangels
Thrones	Powers	Angels

First Hierarchy Choir

This hierarchy is formed by the most pure Angels, the so-called Holy Angels as they are in intimate contact with God/Universe, the creator of all. They are dedicated exclusively to adore, to love and to glorify God/Universe. They are the highest rank of the angelic realm.

Seraphim

This hierarchy is the one closest to the throne of God. They exist in the higher echelons of the hierarchy and their very name means ardour. They are said to encircle the throne, existing off the love emanated by God and they consistently chant, "Holy, holy, holy...". This burning unconditional divine love keeps them forever close to God's Throne and they bear love and light to the lesser choirs of angels. They fill the "cup" of all other angels with the glory and unconditional love of God/Universe.

Cherubim

This hierarchy of angels are second to the seraphim and their name signifies "fullness of knowledge". They are considered to be the guardians and messengers of all the divine mysteries. Their mission and focus is to transmit divine wisdom to all beings. Characterised by having a deep insight into God's secrets and wisdom, the cherubim hold the knowledge of God and they truly possess the fullness of the divine science of heaven. They are sent to earth on very special missions and on very special occasions, when major negative events are about to happen. They enlighten and give guidance to the lesser choirs of angels and they are to them the Voice of Divine Wisdom.

Thrones

This hierarchy of angels hold within themselves the divine essence of God/Universe the Creator and their main task is to pass that grandness to the other Angels. They form the last choir of the first hierarchy which is the closest to the Divine Majesty. They are also known as the Ophanim or Sedes Dei which means "thirsty of God". The primary mission of these angels is to be God's chariot of divine light, but they are also known to carry out God's judgements, by being God's messenger. Their main characteristics are submission and peace, however, they act with impartiality and humility to bring about the desires of God/Universe. God's spirit is conveyed in a certain manner to these angels, who in turn pass on the message to men and the inferior angels.

Second Hierarchy/Choir

This hierarchy are the Angels that have as the primary task of implementing the plan of the divine eternal wisdom. They communicate the plans and projects to the Angels of the third hierarchy that oversee the behaviour of all humankind. They are responsible for all things that happen in the universe, and they ensure that orders are carried out in accordance with God's will, and stopping at all cost outside negative influences.

Dominations

This hierarchy of angels is also known as `Monarchy' because "they rule over all the angelic orders responsible for the execution of the commands of the Great Monarch,

God/Universe." They are also known to be of the highest angelic royalty. The angelic army is obedient to them; their purpose is to regulate the duties of the lower angels. They act as a form of middle management between the upper choir and the lower choir. Receiving their orders from the Seraphim and Cherubim these bright beings of light make known to us the commands of God and ensure the universe remains in order and fully balanced. Their main virtue is zeal for the maintenance of God/Universe authority. Only on very rare occasions do they reveal themselves to mortals. Instead they quietly concern themselves with the details of human existence.

Virtues

This hierarchy of angels ensures that things are done in a perfect and correct way. They also have a mission to remove any obstacles that may interfere with the orders sent by God. They carry out the orders issued by the Dominions and have two main tasks; to maintain the aspects of the natural world, and to bestow blessings upon the material world. Attributed with having strength, their assistance should be sought to combat the enemies of salvation (ie deliverance from harm, ruin, or loss) Their primary duty is to "Preside over the movements of the celestial bodies as well as events of weather including rain, snow, wind and the like". Their secondary duty is to "receive the orders given to them and in turn convert them into miracles for God's favoured". People with spiritual and physical health problems should invoke through prayer these Angels who are Virtues for help and protection.

Powers

This hierarchy of angels are like "Project Managers". It is their main mission to transmit to other Angels in a very special way how things should be done. By the simple fact that they are the ones to delegate God's wishes and commands they are Angels of a very high energetic vibration. They are believed to be "the favourites among human beings". They perform one of the most dangerous tasks, manning the border between Heaven and Earth. Constantly on guard for demonic attacks, their powers act like an elite guard. They are appointed in a special way to fight against the evil spirits, any type of negative energy and to defeat any wicked plans. During heavenly warfare they are a major line of defence.

Third Hierarchy/Choir:

This hierarchy is formed by the Angels that execute the orders of God. They are considered the Angels most close to us human beings and because of this they have a deeper understanding of our nature and of the best way they will be able to assist us. Their main task is to execute with precision the divine will regarding our personal lives by leaving clues, warnings or consequences if that is the case.

Principalities

This hierarchy is the head of the final choir and presides over the third hierarchy. They guide and protect the world's nations, towns and cities, directly watching over the mortal world. They are sent to oversee kings, queens, princes, presidents, ministers and all those in power and to ensure they rule according to God's/Universal law.

Religion and politics are also guarded and monitored by them. As such, they are assumed to be given more freedom to act than the lesser angels below them and are responsible for carrying out divine acts concerning their area of jurisdiction. In addition, they have the task of managing the duties of the third hierarchy angels.

Archangels

This hierarchy consists of very important and special angels. Archangels are entrusted with effecting the more important missions for humankind. They act as leaders of the divine army during battle and protect us under the leadership of Archangel Michael. They are charged with overseeing the duties of all angels in the third choir and at times even the higher choirs. In the past the role of the archangels was not understood by many, but in recent times archangels have established a stronger connection and have calibrated their energies to better communicate with us. As a result there is much more information known with regard to all the archangels, and what their tasks are in providing help to humankind.

Angels

The final group in the last choir in the hierarchy, Angels are ever ready to go wherever the will of God sends them. They have two major tasks. Firstly they are the ordinary messengers sent to men to watch over mortals in a more direct manner than the Principalities. They tend to mirror the goodness of God and direct it toward us. Secondly, they help to protect and keep us safe from negative energies and influences, evil spirits, and demonic attack. Be it households or individual souls, they work with us as guardians and protectors on a daily basis. They are like couriers to both God and the upper angelic hierarchy. They have a strong sense of what is just, good and have a true sense of values. They serve our needs in silence in an extraordinary way. To them serving God in any capacity is a very great honour.

CHAPTER THREE

How Angels Communicate

As servants of God or a loving higher power, angels always send messages to remind us that we are not alone. Angels are not allowed to overwhelm us with their presence though, because that might frighten us and turn us away from angelic communication. Instead, they communicate in subtle ways, using signs, symbols, music, fragrances and daily events to convey messages which will be uniquely meaningful to us.

Angelic language

Here are some of the ways that angels can communicate with us:

⊚ Through special songs that you suddenly tune into on the radio

⊚ With surprising shapes or rainbows in the clouds

⊚ Blissful feeling of Peace, Calm or Warmth

⊚ Tears of joy

⊚ Tingling in the crown area (head)

⊚ Feeling of several hairs being lightly lifted or moved on your head

⊚ A slight breeze

⊚ Pure white feathers appearing

⊚ A cloud shaped like an Angel

- A significant number plate or song

- The approach of a loving animal or child

- Duplicate or recurring numbers e.g. 11.11, 09.09,

- In little sparkles of golden, silvery, or purple light that you might see at the edges of your physical vision

- Through special dreams of castles, rivers, sunlit corridors and other bright places

- Through animals that put in a sudden appearance.

- With moments of synchronicity or 'cosmic coincidences', where something or someone comes your way in a strange but wonderful fashion, providing a message that you alone need to hear.

Pay attention to what is around you, because synchronicities are everywhere.

Communicating with the Angelic Realms

Part 2

CHAPTER FOUR

How to attract Angels into your life

Angels are attracted to joy, happiness and laughter; they love the sound of music, fresh flowers, plants and above all a clean home or work place. You should always shake away any heavy energy before connecting with angels. A very easy way of doing this is to brush down your body with your hands, just like when you brush your hair in the morning, so make a habit of it.

Always be in a positive frame of mind. Here are some elements that will help you connect with the angelic realms:

Colours: Angels just love light colours, pastels, baby colours, especially the Guardian Angels. The colour white is their favourite and the one that the divine messengers of God are especially attracted to. When choosing clothes (including team clothes designs), pictures, or flowers then consider these colours.

Candles: Angels are attracted by coloured candles as they serve as a channel between the angelic realms and us. It is of great importance that you find out what colour candle your Guardian Angel likes, as using that colour will increase the connection with your angel. When lighting the relevant colour for your Guardian Angel, that candle will emanate a specific vibration, and act like a blue print for your private channel of communication. It will also facilitate asking for directions or making your requests.

Clothes: Wearing fresh clean clothes is essential. Angels love cleanliness, and if the clothes are loose, then even better as in this way your aura (energetic field) can flow easily if your angels need to work on you. Remember to wear light coloured clothes even for your underwear when invoking the angelic realms. Angels are very playful, so if you feel like it in your heart you can do a bit of dressing up say like a clown or angel with angel wings. They will be very appreciative. Be childlike when entering the angelic realms, truly you will feel the difference.

Perfumes and Essences: Angels love perfumes and essences - organic ones are the best. As I mentioned above, cleanliness is of the upmost importance. As with your house and work place, keeping your body clean should be a top priority always, as your body is a temple: a temple for the Holy Spirit of the Divine. After your daily hygiene routine, you may use perfume. As with your home, after cleaning your house use incense and invite the Angels into your surroundings. It is very normal to smell roses, lilies and jasmine fragrances when Angels are around. When choosing a perfume or essences go for the ones with a floral bouquet as angels love them; also try your best to have a bouquet of fresh flowers around as they bring high energetic vibrations in to your home or your work place.

Incense: Like candles, incense is a very powerful transmitter when you want to send out your requests and wishes into the angelic realm. Today there are a variety of aromas that have a specific purpose; they are a golden key to connect with Angels. For every angel there is a different fragrance [see Part 3]. For angels generally, the following are examples of incense types that are extremely strong conductors of high energetic angelic vibrations. Using them will open the channel for angels to assist you in different areas of your life.

You can obtain incense either in liquid form and put them in a special incense burner with a tea-light in them or get incense sticks.

Rue: Protects you against negative energies and vibrations and will neutralize/transmute them into positive energy.

Myrrh: In itself is a true blessing and loved by all angels and Archangels, it will bring prosperity, happiness and joy into all areas of your life. My grandmother once said to me that it is powerful to use it before bringing a newborn home as it represents re-birth and its very high vibrations invite battalions of protective angels into the family and home.

Orange: Brings high energetic vibrations and opens the flow in your business/finance life. It also promotes peace harmony and stability in your workplace with all of your co-workers.

Strawberry: A must for those that are prone to Seasonal Affective Disorder (S.A.D.) as it will neutralize emotions related to depression or anxiety. It is also very effective after giving birth both for the mum - as it can help prevent baby blues - and for the baby as it's very calming.

Lotus: This is the diamond of all incenses when it comes to connecting with the spiritual realms, especially when used before and during meditation/visualization, as it harmonizes energies opening the channels to the highest, purest spiritual realms.

Lemon: A true healer of healers, it serves as the catalyst to the body to self-repair and it's very beneficial in promoting good health.

Rosemary: A very powerful conductor, which activates streams of positive energetic vibrations and strengthens positive thoughts.

Cinnamon: This is a little "bedroom" helper as it is a very strong natural aphrodisiac and increases the power of seduction.

Jasmine: Called the incense of pure love, jasmine increases and activates energy of True Love by amplifying the magnetism of the person. A great aide when you are looking for your other half; or you want to re-enforce your relationship.

Rose: Very powerful incense for the ones that truly want to open the channel to pure unconditional love, compassion and mercy.

CHAPTER FIVE

Meet your Guardian Angel

Before we re-incarnate we are assigned a guardian angel. The primary function of a guardian angel is to oversee us throughout our journey in life till the day of our departure from the earth plane. The bond with our guardian is only severed forty-nine to fifty-five days after our passing over to the spiritual realm.

During the journey "home" they stay by our side giving us guidance and protecting us until we fully cross over to the light.

A guardian angel can only intervene with your life if asked to do so from a higher line of command or by our direct request as we have free will and they are bound by our decisions. They protect us and guide us every day of our lives.

The love of your guardian angel is unconditional divine love. No matter what your actions, your angel will always love you, you can be very sure of that, but your angel will always try his/her utmost to guide you onto the right path in life, the path of truth and honour in alignment with God/Universe.

Your Guardian Angel is a pure celestial being of light and should be addressed with the utmost respect and pure kindness. Invoke your guardian angel in times of need with kind gentle words and a lower tone of voice. Assign tasks for your angel to do. Angels just love to get on with work, but if you don't ask your guardian angel, and/or other angels to support and assist you, i.e., giving them your consent, they cannot help. As much as your angel would love to just get on with the job, there are spiritual laws that cannot be broken There is no bending of the rules or taking short cuts when working with the angelic realms, on the contrary following them will guide you into a path of truth, honour and integrity.

Your guardian angel is eager to present him or herself to you so you are able to create a true bond. For that to happen you need to want it and ask for it, then just say to your angel that you would love to deeply connect and to know him/her at a deeper level, it is as simple as that.

So let's start asking:

"My dear beloved guardian angel, I call upon you now with an open heart and ask that you make yourself known to me. My greatest wish is for us to have a deeper connection; I want to feel you in my heart today and every day of my life, walking by your side the same way you have been walking by mine. I open my heart now to connect with you in whatever form, you see fit and always for my highest good.

In love and light, love and light, love and the purest divine Celestial light."

CHAPTER SIX

Connecting with Archangels and Angels

It is obvious to all of us that only the messengers of God
can give us that special help so needed in moments of
hardship. These amazing celestial beings form a strong
link between mankind and God/Source/spirit; they are the
bridge between the physical realm and the divine
spiritual realms.

Many people are unsure how to connect with Angels,
how to communicate and ask for their help. It's easy and
very simple, but there are some new rules to follow as a
result of changing energies and vibration of the planet:

⊘ To truly connect with the angelic realms it is
extremely important to open your heart, believe and trust
that angels are as real as you and me, then simply invite
them into your life. Angels are as pure as a child and they
are connected with everything that is good, happy, jolly
and beautiful.

⊘ To connect to your angel first choose a calm and
peaceful place where you can completely relax and be
undisturbed. You can choose to sit or lie on the floor and
just open your heart so you are better able to
understand/feel the energies sent by the angelic realm.

⊘ Start by clearing your mind and opening your
heart space by deep breathing. Breathe out your

concerns, worries and all that is on your mind and breathe in balance, peace and harmony before connecting with the spiritual realms is of the utmost importance. Breathe in and out deeply five times and relax your mind. If you feel the need to do it for longer just go with your feelings and intuition and do so.

◎ As soon as you feel relaxed, take a moment to do a heartfelt prayer, speak to your angel as you would converse with a best friend. In fact your angels are truly your best friends, so pour your heart out to them. This is also fundamental for creating a deep connection.

◎ Start a conversation: ask your angel to calm you down in moments of stress and worry, to guide you and inspire you in your moments of doubt, and to strengthen your faith, but never forget to thank your angel for all that he/she is doing for you. Just open and pour your heart out to him/her. When you truly connect with angels I can assure you, you will never feel low [or loneliness] in your life.

◎ Open your heart: when you close your heart to love, happiness, joy or sweet words, Angels have difficulty in connecting. Even in moments of sadness remember and bring forward your most happy moments. This way the Angels will transmute negative emotions into purity and joy.

◎ Other than your Guardian Angel, in accordance with the angelic hierarchy, and taking into consideration your present situation, another specific Angel may come to help. For example archangels are responsible for following God's command during special assignments.

◎ It is important to understand how to ask and see in context how important the problem that you are experiencing in your life is. It is not really appropriate to ask for help with very minor matters!

❧ Showing respect and kindness for the angelic realm is fundamental for a good line of communication. Be kind and gentle when communicating, using tender loving words.

❧ Most important of all, understand that the angelic realm is pure divine light, pure unconditional divine love, so you should only invoke angels for actions of pure goodness. They are here to protect us, to guide us in our daily lives, to oversee our difficulties, concerns and emotional setbacks and never in any way or form to cause harm to another human being. Remember, even simple negative thoughts will bring major karma and consequences to you.

❧ As soon as you receive the blessing from your request to the angelic realm, is very important to acknowledge it and to express thanks with all your heart. Many people are fast to ask but extremely late to be grateful for the blessings that they have received.

❧ If you feel it in your heart, you can have a little altar dedicated to your Angel, a special place that you create and dedicate to him and where you will "anchor" your Guardian Angel to you and your home.

CHAPTER SEVEN

Invoking Archangels and Angels

To invoke an angel or archangel, first say the angel's name three times, then either ask the angel to be with you. Alternatively make a specific request for help with whatever you are doing, or to help someone else. Then complete the invocation by saying the words: "In love and light" three times, signifying that your intent is honest. For example, to invoke Archangel Michael (angel of strength, protection and truth) you can say:

"Michael, Michael, Michael, please be with me now to (your request) in loving white light of the God of Love, Truth and Life. In Love and Light, Love and Light, Love and Light. Thank You".

Close your eyes to monitor the response of the angels this might feel like tingling or tickling energy, warmth, or a cool breeze on the palms, fingers (usually starting in the left, or taking hand) or around your heart. Sometimes it is felt on the head or body, flowing down the arms or legs. You may get a perfume or scent that comes and goes, or you may see visions or colours.

Whatever you receive, always remember to thank the angels for their help afterwards. It may be that you are new to all this and don't feel much to begin with. If this is the case, I urge you to persevere, as the response feels stronger with practice and patience! This is because as you continue to do these invocations, your own vibration level and frequency will gradually rise, getting closer to that of the angels, and enhancing your ability to feel.

CHAPTER EIGHT

The Anchorage of your Guardian Angel

A guardian angel is an angelic being of light, which walks with an individual throughout their time on Earth as a guide and protector. Everyone has one: your guardian angel is assigned to you at conception.

The anchorage process "anchors" your guardian angel to you, so he or she is always around. Doing the anchorage and candles for your guardian angel helps build your rapport with your spirit guides and your guardian angel. Angels, and especially our guardian angel, are our protection, our first line of defence, so it is important to keep them strong. Angels 'feed' on light, candles, faith, good feelings, and prayers. The more you feed them, the more they work for you. This is why it is so important to do regular candles for your guardian angel.

We use candles to symbolise our faith through the flames. In the flame of a candle, all the forces of nature are activated. The lit candle symbolises the individualisation of ascending life and the light of the soul. We can shift our lives with meditation and angel candles alone.

The anchorage of the guardian angel is divine science, alchemy. To be successful you need to concentrate on the power of your mind and your will. The anchorage is a process, where you anchor your guardian angel into your home and tell him or her, what each coloured candle stands for. This is a kind of 'programming' of your angel and is done by lighting specific candles at a specific time every day for one week. After the anchorage your angel is ready to work.

You need to start the anchorage on a Monday and light a candle each day in the order of the colours given below. It is important to do the candles at the time of day of your angel - the same time every day. If that is not possible (e.g. due to work commitments), do it as closely to that time as possible and apologise and explain it to your guardian angel.

You will need to start your anchorage with a blue candle on a Monday and finish with a violet candle on the following Sunday. The anchorage is only complete once the last candle has finished burning and you have scattered its ashes. For more information on how to do the candles please see the step-by-step guide on page 68.

On the last day, just after lighting your candle, do the energetic cleansing of your home with the help of your angels.

During the week of the anchorage, your angel will show you what colour candles you need more of by the position of the wick once the candle has finished burning. So take notes and pictures of how the candles and the wick look after they finish burning. If the wick is pointing 'down' (meaning 6pm or towards it, or down as in vertically down) you need to light more candles of that colour after the anchorage. Do a set of three candles of each of those colours after you have completed the anchorage see below for further details on how to do a set of candles.

Candle Colours

During the week of the anchorage, don't ask, order or invoke your angel to do anything. Simply tell them what each colour stands for, and that it's for you and your life only. It's like inserting a new program on your computer. After you have completed the anchorage, you can start making requests to your guardian angel.

The sequence for the candles to be lit during the anchorage process is:

1st day: Blue candle for spiritual cleanliness, faith, strength, power, money, business, work.

2nd day: Yellow candle for sharpening intelligence, wisdom, justice, communication, changes, financial exchanges.

3rd day: Pink candle to strengthen relationships based on love and affection and to activate the interior flame of your twin soul. It is the most perfect colour. You can use it whenever you need to emanate good energy for somebody.

4th day: White candle for harmony, peace, equilibrium, and ascension. It removes the contrary angel. (For the best results recite Psalm 91 as you light it followed by your angel's psalm and move your fingers with the oil on the candle away from your heart).

5th day: Green candle for physical health, abundance, truth, and calm.

6th day: Red candle for protection and emergency situations. Also for dynamism, strength, and courage.

7th day: Violet candle which represents transmutation. It transforms negative energy into positive energy. It also stands for freedom and spirituality.

Preparation

Guardian Angel name

Find out the name of your guardian angel in Chapter Nine, or my website www.lidiafrederico.com under the 'Angels' link.

Time

It is important that you do the anchorage in your home and on consecutive days over one week. So you need a week where you can light a candle every day at your home starting on Monday and finishing on Sunday.

Place

Ideally create something like an altar or sacred space where you can light your candles. Candles for guardian angels and spirits of light will have to be lit and left approximately 60-90cm off the floor - e.g. a kitchen worktop, table or shelf and not on the ground (as they are superior beings).

It is best if this place is also the place you pray and meditate; a calm and isolated place where you will not be disturbed. It is important that you always do your 'rituals' (meditation, prayer, candles etc.) in the same place - especially for the week of the angel anchorage. This way, the place will become impregnated with your energy, the sacred place of your proper heart and the Universe.

You might want to place incense, crystals and everything you use for your meditations in this place. Keep it clean, tidy and pretty and separate from other people's glasses, plates and candles. As with all spiritual tools and items and all things you bring into your house, touch the top of the item, in this case the candle, and ask God/Universe to take all negative energies away and to bless it.

If possible, salt wash the plate (not the glass or goblet) before its first use. Do this by mixing 3 handfuls of sea salt with your right hand into water until the salt is dissolved and soak the plate in it for 24 hours. After that, wash and dry it as normal. Cleanse your angel plates and glasses like this approximately every 6 months or whenever necessary.

Wash and clean your plate and glass before each use or candle ritual, just as you would with your plate used for eating from. If you use a hurricane glass or funnel, wash it after every one or two uses.

Reserve these items for spiritual use only. Do not eat from your angel plate or cook with the consecrated oil. Should this happen by accident, either buy a new virgin plate or glass or salt wash it again before using it. Keep these items out of reach and sight of others when not in use.

Lay the table for the angel to 'eat' in the same way you would set the table for a person to eat. Place the clean virgin plate down and position the glass (or goblet) filled with fresh clean water on the right hand side of the plate before lighting a candle. The water serves to drain and trap negative energy from the environment. If bubbles appear adhered to the walls of the glass it signals negative energies have been cleansed. In some cases the water even gets dirty or muddy.

Put a fresh red apple next to the plate and glass and replace it when needed, i.e. as soon as it starts going brown and wrinkly. Dispose of the old apple in nature, in the same way you would with the leftover wax. Apples have a very strong energy in their interior.

Angel anchorage template

For each candle you need to prepare your angel anchorage template. For the week of the anchorage it is important to use golden paper. Afterwards, golden paper is still the best, but you can also use good quality plain white paper.

Cut out the angel template. Inside this circle, draw by hand with a blue or green pen, two overlapping circles with cross symbols as shown, and write your name, your angel's and archangel's names in the places specified.

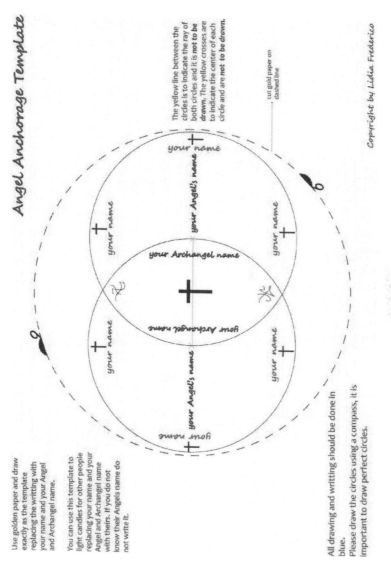

Angel Anchorage Template

The yellow line between the circles is to indicate the ray of both circles and it is **not to be drawn**. The yellow crosses are to indicate the center of each circle and are **not to be drawn**.

cut gold paper on dashed line

your name

your Angel's name

your name

your Archangel name

your name

your Archangel name

your name

your Angel's name

your name

Use golden paper and draw exactly as the template replacing the writting with your name and your Angel and Archangel name.

You can use this template to light candles for other people replacing your name and your Angel and Archangel name with theirs. If you do not know their Angels name do not write it.

All drawing and writting should be done in blue.
Please draw the circles using a compass, it is important to draw perfect circles.

You can prepare the templates (see diagram) in advance. In fact, it is a good idea to always have a few ready in case you need to do a candle at short notice.

You can also write your intention or wish on the back of the paper, phrasing it as positively as possible. For example: to move the contrary angel away from my life, and find a new job which is in my highest good. Do this just before lighting the candle.

Light candles with a match, never with another candle or a lighter. Incense sticks are best lit with a candle, rather than a match and especially not with a lighter. Never blow on them to extinguish the flame; wave them in the air.

Tip: you might want to use a napkin or do the candle topless to avoid getting oil on your blouse or shirt.

Checklist – you will need:

- Virgin white plate
- Hand drawn angel template (write in blue or green ink)
- Goblet or glass of clean water (it should be crystal due to its high energetic vibration)
- Virgin olive oil
- Virgin candle of choice
- Unlit incense
- Matches
- Glass funnel or Hurricane for wind protection (optional)
- Any special prayers that you want to recite
- A red apple

Step-by-step guide

๑ Wear comfortable clothes and wash your hands (or shower).

๑ Clear your mind, release any negative energies, or meditate for a few minutes in the space near to your altar or other calm and isolated place that you use for rituals.

๑ Relax and focus on what you want to achieve. Visualise your wish as if it had already come true and from a good source of energy (and not where you are now) so it is a different energy that your wish comes from.

๑ Get up and stand in front of your altar or ritual space.

๑ Place your right hand over your goblet or glass of clean, fresh, water and bless the water.

๑ You could say something like this:

"God, please bless this water so that it absorbs all negative energy from around and within this space leaving it pure and clean. In love and light. Blessed be."

๑ Mentally recite one or several of the following:

- the psalm of your guardian angel (for the anchorage say 1-5 of your psalm, afterwards just the 1st part is fine)
- your guardian angel prayer(s)
- The Lord's Prayer or other prayers of choice according to your spiritual beliefs.

❂ You can repeat these several times to strengthen your blessing.

❂ Pick up the candle and hold it up in two hands as an offering to your guardian angel saying something like this replacing xxxxxx with the relevant name, colour and request:

"Guardian angel, xxxxxx. I offer this xxxxx coloured candle to you with a request for xxxxxx. In love and light. Blessed be, Amen."

Add some drops of the olive oil to the thumb and index finger of your right hand and anoint the candle by placing its base against your heart with the wick at the top of the candle pointing outwards, away from your body. Draw the oil along the candle with your finger and thumb towards yourself three times, rotating the candle as you do so, so that the oil covers the candle. As you are doing this, say:

"Blessed be my wish because now it is coming true."

❂ If you want to *receive* a blessing, e.g. more faith, draw the fingers with the oil *towards* your heart. When you want to *remove* something from your life, e.g. the contrary angel, draw your fingers, with the oil on them, from the base of the candle, positioned on your heart *away* from yourself towards the wick at the top of the candle three times.

So either draw the oil towards or away from your heart according to your wish. If you want something coming in your life, draw the oil in, and if you want something coming out of your life, draw it out.

۞   Take the candle between the palms of your hands and energise it by rubbing or rolling it gently. Visualise your wish manifesting (coming true) as you do this. Do this with an internal attitude of faith and confidence.

۞   Light the candle with a match. Never use a lighter, and never burn the base of the candle.

۞   Use the top of the candle to drip wax onto the virgin white plate.

۞   Place your angel template on top of the melted wax and fix it down in the middle of the plate.

۞   Add some more drops of wax to the centre of your angel map and secure the candle on top of it. Make sure the candle is right in the centre, where the two circles overlap.

۞   Say this word three times: "Momentum."

۞   Place the glass funnel over the candle, if you are using one.

۞   Thank your guardian angel. You can say your angel's psalm again or any of your chosen prayers if you feel it in your heart to do so.

۞   Leave the candle to burn right down until it goes out by itself. Under no circumstances blow the candle out. If the candle extinguishes, do not light it again. You will need to do a new candle.

۞   You can light incense from the candle to bless and protect your sacred space or altar, and energetically clean your house with your angel's incense. After lighting your candle, listen to it and watch the flame. You can also light it and be connected to your angel whilst you are doing other things.

◎   If the candle burns a little or all of the paper by itself, say: "Momentum, momentum, momentum".

◎   When the candle has finished burning, look at the pattern of wax that has formed and the way the wick is positioned. What can you see? Do any images form?

◎   Carefully take the wax off the paper and plate and place in a special box. At the end of the week, take them to a place in nature such as the base of a large tree or beneath some shrubs in your garden. Ask for the elements (fire, air, earth and water) to take care of your wishes and say "momentum" 3 times. After the anchorage you can do this either after each candle or collect the wax and dispose of it every Friday in nature.

Never throw any leftovers of candles down the toilet or in the bin, otherwise your wish will be going down the toilet or in the bin.

The candle should have burnt the paper a little. If not, once you have moved the candle wax residue, you need to burn all the remaining paper with a match.

Crumble the paper ash into dust using your right hand fingers and blow them into the wind outside the front of your house (from your front door or main window facing the front of your house) and as you scatter the ashes say "momentum, momentum, momentum". Do this as soon as possible after the candle has finished burning, as the paper contains the essence of the angel.

Look at the water in your goblet or glass. If it is clear, drink it within 24 hours. If it has been there for longer than 24 hours, water the plants with it. Or if bubbles have formed it means negative energy has been trapped in the water. So instead of drinking it, water the plants with it and ask for the negative energy to be transformed into positive and neutral energies.

Messages from your angel in candles

Look closely at the shape of the remaining wax or the hole that was burnt in the paper for any images which might give you a message (e.g. a sad or happy face).

When the candle has finished burning, check which way the wick is pointing (as if on a clock face):

◐   *Good:* pointing in the upper half of the clock face i.e. between 9 and 3 o'clock, ideally at 12 o'clock

◐   *Not so good:* lower half = 3-9 o'clock, worst: 6 o'clock (meaning your Angel needs another candle in regards to this matter).

The direction of the candle can give you additional detail information as follows: a wick pointing to the left side (around 9 o'clock) indicates issues to address regarding relationships, emotions, and/or your heart. A wick pointing to the right side (around 3 o'clock) indicates issues around material things or money.

If your wick points to the material side but you have asked something regarding matters of the heart, it means you did not ask from your heart but had another, ulterior motive. So you will need to light another candle for this wish.

If the wick was pointing down, ask your angel to show you in your dreams what this was about and what you need to do.

Other indications:

⊙   Wick divides in two: the request was made in the wrong way.

⊙   Tip of the wick is shiny: you will have much luck and success with your request.

⊙   Candle does not light: the angel may be having difficulties anchoring. You may have negative energies around you.

⊙   Candle burning with a bluish light: it indicates the presence of angels and archangels - a very good sign.

⊙   Flame is vacillating (wavering, flickering): the angel is demonstrating that, due to some circumstances, what was requested will have some changes.

⊙   Flame looks like fireworks and sends sparks into the air: the angel will place somebody in your path to give you guidance. You will have some type of disappointment before your request is carried through.

⊙   Flame seems to spiral: your request will be met; the angel is already working on the message.

⊙   Candle that cries and hisses too much: the angel is having difficulties in carrying through your request.

⊙   Very little wax and wick is left: the angel needs more candles for that aspect or more emotions when you light the candle.

After the anchorage

After you have completed the guardian angel anchorage, which is a kind of programming, your angel is ready to work.

From then on you need to light a candle for your guardian angel every 3 days, meaning on the 4th day at the latest.

For example, if you lit a candle on Monday you need to do the next one on Friday the latest.

It is very important to do candles regularly as they strengthen and feed your guardian angel and (s)he is your main protection. You eat, so why shouldn't your angel 'eat'?

A skinny angel doesn't work and protect properly. If you are unable to do a candle every 3 days (e.g. if you are travelling), ask a friend who has completed their anchorage to do a candle for you.

If you or someone around you drops a knife or fork and it nearly misses you or it sticks in the floor (blade/forks down), it means your guardian angel needs feeding urgently, and also that he or she trying to communicate something very important to you.

During the anchorage it is very important to do your candle at a specific time of day. After the anchorage, it is still best to do your candle at the time of your guardian angel or at angel times. These are hours where any spiritual or energy work is very powerful and effective. Apart from the specific time relevant to your own Guardian Angel, angel candles, prayers, and meditations are best done at 3am/pm, and 9am/pm.

You can also light your candle at other times of the day as long as it is not around the 'Silence Hours' as I call them: avoid the hours of 5.45- 6.15am/pm and 11.45-12.15am/pm. Ideally, do at least one or two candles a week at the guardian angel's particular time. You might want to do a candle just before you go into a busy place or energetically heavy environment (e.g. a nightclub), so your candle is burning while you are there.

It is very important to leave at least 24 hours between lighting one candle and the next, otherwise you over charge your angel. This applies to candles for the same person as well. It is fine, however, to do a candle for yourself and one for someone else at the same time.

During the anchorage, you programmed your angel to understand what each colour stands for. Now, after the anchorage, use candles for wishes or specific issues you need help with and ask your guardian angel to show you messages in the candles. The act of lighting a candle for the guardian angel is a way of activating your wish or request and taking it to the universal plane.

Go to your chart and see which colour is appropriate for what's happening in your life, use your intuition and let your angel talk to you. Pick the colours you feel drawn to or guided to. Make sure you do at least one white candle a week to move the contrary angel away from your life. Ensure you do all colours approximately every two weeks, and at least once a month.

If you open a spiritual fast, it is highly recommended to light a white candle or a set of 3 white candles, on or before the 1st day of fasting, to remove the contrary angel from your life. See the section below for guidelines on how to prepare a set of candles and chapter 18 for more information on the contrary angel.

Visualise your wish before and whilst lighting the candle.

Focus on what you want as if it was already there and not where you are now so your wish is coming from that different positive energy place.

Set of 3 or 7 candles *(Preparation)*

You might be asked to, or feel guided to, do a set of candles.

Usually this is for something serious or important. In this case, light a candle of the same colour each day for 3 or 7 days in a row with the same wish. It is important that you do the candles at the same time every day at your angel's time or 'angel time'. The same rules as for the anchorage apply. Alternatively, you can find a bigger candle of the relevant colour that will burn for 3 or 7 days. For example, if your problem is you want a better job, light seven blue candles for 7 days in a row or one 7 day duration candle.

Lighting candles for other people:

Only do this if you have permission from the person. You can only do this once you have completed your angel anchorage, after scattering the ashes of the paper circle of the 7th candle on the Sunday. Only light candles inside your home for people who are still alive.

Make sure you have a plate and glass that is uniquely for your guardian angel. Ideally have 1 or 2 other sets of angel glasses and plates for use on behalf of others.

Follow the same process as lighting a candle for yourself and write the person's name and angels' names on the paper. If you don't know their angels' names, simply write their name and leave the rest blank. If the water does not have any or very few bubbles, and it's convenient, give it to the person you did the candle for to drink or water plants with it.

Light the candle with pure feelings in your heart - the stronger and purer your feelings are, the stronger the candle's effect. Feel deeply in your heart and devote several minutes to it for the benefit of the person you are lighting the candle for. Be truthful, do it from your heart, with no ulterior motives, not expecting recognition or gratitude...then do it!

Notes if lighting more than one candle at a time:

Candles, especially spiritual candles, need to be always lit in uneven numbers: 3, 5, 7 and so on. This is because candles lit in pairs cancel out the energy of the other candle. You can light candles at different times, as long as you always light enough to create an uneven number.

For example, if you lit one candle earlier, you can light more whilst the first one is burning or has been burning for a while as long as it makes an uneven number. For example: if you lit one candle at 2pm, and did another one at 5pm, you also need to light a 3rd one at 5pm. You can simply light a small tea light to make up the required odd number of candles (i.e. the tea-light is the third candle in this case). It is fine if the candles burn out at different times.

If you had an important request and your guardian angel has not replied to you within 14 days, light a white candle for your archangel on your angel plate. If your archangel does not reply within 14 days, ask if your request was for your highest good and wait to be shown. Some requests take longer than others.

If you want to get slimmer, hold your hand above the glass of water before you light your candle and ask your guardian angel to bless it so that when you drink the water it will flush out all excess fat from your body.

Remember to talk to your guardian angel regularly, like saying prayers in your head. He or she is your friend.

Meeting and deeply connecting with your Guardian Angel

Part 3

CHAPTER NINE

Guardian Angels Calendar

To find the name of your Guardian Angel, select the day of your birth in the relevant month. You can also search for family, friends and loved ones. Once found please go to Chapter 10 to source all the information there.

January		
01 - Rochel	11 - Lelahel	21 - Hekamiah
02 - Yabamiah	12 - Achaiah	22 - Lauviah
03 - Haiaiel	13 - Cahethel	23 - Caliel
04 - Mumiah	14 - Haziel	24 - Leuviah
05 - Angel of Humanity	15 - Aladiah	25 - Pahaliah
06 - Vehuiah	16 - Laoviah	26 - Nelchael
07 - Jeliel	17 - Hahahiah	27 - Ieiaiel
08 - Sitael	18 - Yesalel	28 - Melahel
09 - Elemiah	19 - Mebahel	29 - Haheuiah
10 - Mahasiah	20 - Hariel	30 - Nith-Haiah
		31 - Haaiah

February

February		
01 - Ierathel	11 - Aniel	21 - Asaliah
02 - Seheiah	12 - Haamiah	22 - Mihael
03 - Reyel	13 - Rehael	23 - Vehuel
04 - Omael	14 - Ieiazel	24 - Daniel
05 - Lecabel	15 - Hahahel	25 - Hahasiah
06 - Vasahiah	16 - Mikael	26 - Imamaiah
07 - Iehuiah	17 - Veuliah	27 - Nanael
08 - Lehahiah	18 - Yelaiah	28 - Nithael
09 - Chavakiah	19 - Sealiah	29 - Nithael
10 - Menadel	20 - Ariel	

March

March		
01 - Mebahiah	11 - Damabiah	21 - Jeliel
02 - Poiel	12 - Manakel	22 - Sitael
03 - Nemamiah	13 - Ayel	23 - Elemiah
04 - Ieialel	14 - Habuhiah	24 - Mahasiah
05 - Harahel	15 - Rochel	25 - Lelahel
06 - Mitzrael	16 - Yabamiah	26 - Achaiah
07 - Umabel	17 - Haiaiel	27 - Cahethel
08 - Iah-hel	18 - Mumiah	28 - Haziel
09 - Anauel	19 - Angel of Humanity	29 - Aladiah
10 - Mehiel	20 - Vehuiah	30 - Laoviah
		31 - Hahahiah

April		
01 - Yesalel	11 - Melahel	21 - Iehuiah
02 - Mebahel	12 - Haheuiah	22 - Lehahiah
03 - Hariel	13 - Nith-Haiah	23 - Chavakiah
04 - Hekamiah	14 - Haaiah	24 - Menadel
05 - Lauviah	15 - Ierathel	25 - Aniel
06 - Caliel	16 - Seheiah	26 - Haamiah
07 - Leuviah	17 - Reyel	27 - Rehael
08 - Pahaliah	18 - Omael	28 - Ieiazel
09 - Nelchael	19 - Lecabel	29 - Hahahel
10 - Ieiaiel	20 - Vasahiah	30 - Mikael

May		
01 - Veuliah	11 - Nanael	21 - Anauel
02 - Yelaiah	12 - Nithael	22 - Mehiel
03 - Sealiah	13 - Mebahiah	23 - Damabiah
04 - Ariel	14 - Poiel	24 - Manakel
05 - Asaliah	15 - Nemamiah	25 - Ayel
06 - Mihael	16 - Ieialel	26 - Habuhiah
07 - Vehuel	17 - Harahel	27 - Rochel
08 - Daniel	18 - Mitzrael	28 - Yabamiah
09 - Hahasiah	19 - Umabel	29 - Haiaiel
10 - Imamaiah	20 - Iah-hel	30 - Mumiah
		31 - Angel of Humanity

June		
01 - Vehuiah	11 - Laoviah	21 - Nelchael
02 - Jeliel	12 - Hahahiah	22 - Ieiaiel
03 - Sitael	13 - Yesalel	23 - Melahel
04 - Elemiah	14 - Mebahel	24 - Haheuiah
05 - Mahasiah	15 - Hariel	25 - Nith-Haiah
06 - Lelahel	16 - Hekamiah	26 - Haaiah
07 - Achaiah	17 - Lauviah	27 - Ierathel
08 - Cahethel	18 - Caliel	28 - Seheiah
09 - Haziel	19 - Leuviah	29 - Reyel
10 - Aladiah	20 - Pahaliah	30 - Omael

July		
01 - Lecabel	11 - Hahahel	21 - Hahasiah
02 - Vasahiah	12 - Mikael	22 - Imamaiah
03 - Iehuiah	13 - Veuliah	23 - Nanael
04 - Lehahiah	14 - Yelaiah	24 - Nithael
05 - Chavakiah	15 - Sealiah	25 - Mebahiah
06 - Menadel	16 - Ariel	26 - Poiel
07 - Aniel	17 - Asaliah	27 - Nemamiah
08 - Haamiah	18 - Mihael	28 - Ieialel
09 - Rehael	19 - Vehuel	29 - Harahel
10 - Ieiazel	20 - Daniel	30 - Mitzrael
		31 - Umabel

August		
01 - Iah-hel	11 - Mumiah	21 - Haziel
02 - Anauel	12 - Angel of Humanity	22 - Aladiah
03 - Mehiel	13 - Vehuiah	23 - Laoviah
04 - Damabiah	14 - Jeliel	24 - Hahahiah
05 - Manakel	15 - Sitael	25 - Yesalel
06 - Ayel	16 - Elemiah	26 - Mebahel
07 - Habuhiah	17 - Mahasiah	27 - Hariel
08 - Rochel	18 - Lelahel	28 - Hekamiah
09 - Yabamiah	19 - Achaiah	29 - Lauviah
10 - Haiaiel	20 - Cahethel	30 - Caliel
		31 - Leuviah

September		
01 - Pahaliah	11 - Omael	21 - Ieiazel
02 - Nelchael	12 - Lecabel	22 - Hahahel
03 - Ieiaiel	13 - Vasahiah	23 - Mikael
04 - Melahel	14 - Iehuiah	24 - Veuliah
05 - Haheuiah	15 - Lehahiah	25 - Yelaiah
06 - Nith-Haiah	16 - Chavakiah	26 - Sealiah
07 - Haaiah	17 - Menadel	27 - Ariel
08 - Ierathel	18 - Aniel	28 - Asaliah
09 - Seheiah	19 - Haamiah	29 - Mihael
10 - Reyel	20 - Rehael	30 - Vehuel

October		
01 - Daniel	11 - Mitzrael	21 - Yabamiah
02 - Hahasiah	12 - Umabel	22 - Haiaiel
03 - Imamaiah	13 - Iah-hel	23 - Mumiah
04 - Nanael	14 - Anauel	24 - Angel of Humanity
05 - Nithael	15 - Mehiel	25 - Vehuiah
06 - Mebahiah	16 - Damabiah	26 - Jeliel
07 - Poiel	17 - Manakel	27 - Sitael
08 - Nemamiah	18 - Ayel	28 - Elemiah
09 - Ieialel	19 - Habuhiah	29 - Mahasiah
10 - Harahel	20 - Rochel	30 - Lelahel
		31 - Achaiah

November		
01 - Cahethel	11 - Caliel	21 - Seheiah
02 - Haziel	12 - Leuviah	22 - Reyel
03 - Aladiah	13 - Pahaliah	23 - Omael
04 - Laoviah	14 - Nelchael	24 - Lecabel
05 - Hahahiah	15 - Ieiaiel	25 - Vasahiah
06 - Yesalel	16 - Melahel	26 - Iehuiah
07 - Mebahel	17 - Haheuiah	27 - Lehahiah
08 - Hariel	18 - Nith-Haiah	28 - Chavakiah
09 - Hekamiah	19 - Haaiah	29 - Menadel
10 - Lauviah	20 - Ierathel	30 - Aniel

December		
01 - Haamiah	11 - Mihael	21 - Ieialel
02 - Rehael	12 - Vehuel	22 - Harahel
03 - Ieiazel	13 - Daniel	23 - Mitzrael
04 - Hahahel	14 - Hahasiah	24 - Umabel
05 - Mikael	15 - Imamaiah	25 - Iah-hel
06 - Veuliah	16 - Nanael	26 - Anauel
07 - Yelaiah	17 - Nithael	27 - Mehiel
08 - Sealiah	18 - Mebahiah	28 - Damabiah
09 - Ariel	19 - Poiel	29 - Manakel
10 - Asaliah	20 - Nemamiah	30 - Ayel
		31 - Habuhiah

CHAPTER TEN

Who is your Guardian Angel?

According to the day of our birth, we all have a special angel who protects and accompanies us throughout our lives, and that somehow influences the characteristics of the individual via their personality. The angels always stimulate our virtues and qualities, but at times we will often choose to vibrate and/or act negatively, tuning in and opening the doors for our contrary angel to influence our daily life. The contrary angel acts as if it were our evil angel sitting on one of our shoulders, with the good angel on the other side, just like in the cartoons. This scenario happens very often if we are not mindful and most of the time we are unaware of it.

So it is important to know the features of our guardian angel to strengthen them and form an alliance, thereby achieving living positively and harmoniously with God and those around us, as well as grounding and anchoring.

Each angel has a specific day of the week and specific hour in which he or she acts more strongly due to planetary alignments, or when he or she is closer to us in the terrestrial earth plane. It is more beneficial to do prayers and requests to our guardian angel at these days and at these times, in order to more easily tune into their energy. In addition, each angel has a candle colour, psalm and crystal which if you prefer to use them, helps immensely with your "anchorage" because the energy of those elements is very similar to your angel's vibration.

The following pages list a summary of the main features of each guardian angel and their anchorages acting elements.

ACHAIAH
Protects days: 12/01 - 07/07 - 19/08 - 31/10

Invoke this angel to have more patience. Achaiah facilitates the discovery of the secrets of nature and influences the propagation of light at work.

Influence: Those born under the influence of Angel Achaiah are very spiritual, yet at the same time they have their feet on the floor, look at the horizon and have their mind on the stars. Even if they are without opportunities of education, they are very knowledgeable and will have great influence. People born under this angel's protection are tenacious, dogged and have a huge need to know all sides of an issue. They always aim not to miss any opportunity. Having spiritual protection through their intuition allows them to take risks. Someone under Achaiah's influence will be unselfish, immensely patient and understanding with everything and everyone. They are extremely sensitive when in contact with plants, animals or even the human brain and apply the knowledge of nature in designing machinery.

Professionally: Anyone born under the influence of Achaiah can be successful as an artist working for television, film or working with producers in editing videos or movies. Their work is marked by originality and the use of technology in the dissemination of art. They may work in marketing new equipment or in microcomputers, media systems, precision technology or their repair.

Contrary Angel: This contrary angel is the enemy of light and dominates negligence, apathy, laziness and inconsistency in studying. Those dominated by this contrary angel may be stagnant, stopped, not face difficulties or fulfill their promises, have no altruism or generosity. Be understanding when you have evidence in your hands. They may be part of a militant political party that exploits violence and may struggle to speak and be understood. Closed in their little world that appears attractive, people under the influence of this angel do not realise their decadence.

Hierarchy: Seraphim
Archangel: Metatron
Planet: Mercury
Power number: 10
Month of change: October
Is present on Earth: from 2:00am to 2:20am
Incense: Orange Blossom or Lavender
Weekday: Friday
Colour of Candle: LightYellow
Crystal: Hemetite
Psalm: 102, verse 8

"My enemies reproach me all day. Those who are mad at me use my name as a curse."

ALADIAH
Protects days: 15/01 - 29/03 - 10/6 - 22/08 - 03/11

Invoke this angel to help against diseases and evil.

Influence: Those born under Aladiah's influence have a good heart, be high in integrity, spend time in good company and have a busy social life. They are angels on earth, reserved and dedicated to their beloved. People under this angel's protection are endowed with great imagination, self confidence, flexibility and the ability to always choose the best path or opportunity. They work hard and will spare no efforts to make everyone live in a fairer society. Being in harmony, they understand nature and the cycles of life. They take good care of their body, because their motto is "healthy mind in healthy body".

Professionally: Anyone born under Aladiah's influence can make a success working in medicine, hospitals, psychiatry, social work, nursing, pharmaceutical or herbal medicine. They have a fertile imagination, so their hobby may be writing detective novels, imaginary or fictitious stories, surprising others with accuracy of their facts.

Contrary Angel: Someone dominated by this angel may have an inclination to inhibition, infidelity, neglect of health or business or the tendency to abuse drugs, alcohol or tobacco. They may not know to use their strength, might cover up crimes, or deal with or be receivers of contraband.

Hierarchy: Cherubim
Archangel: Haziel
Planet: Mercury
Power number: 5
Month of Change: May
Is present on Earth: from 3:00am to 3:20 am
Incense: Lavander
Colour of Candle: Green
Weekday: Monday
Crystal: Amazonite
Psalm: 32, verse 2

"Blessed is the man to whom Yahweh doesn't impute iniquity, in whose spirit there is no deceit."

ANAUEL

Protects days: 09/03 - 21/05 - 08/02 - 14/10 - 26/12

Invoke this angel to help you find true spirituality and gain wisdom. Anauel protects against health problems and accidents, keeps the peace in families and counteracts the evil of enemies.

Influence: Those born under the influence of this angel will be of subtle spirit, shrewd, inventive and distinguished by their work. They will be eager for knowledge and have an appreciation for studies and reading. Their conscience will turn into real words and actions. Understanding the mysteries of the link between all things, someone under Anauel's protection will be a great light on earth, acting as the perfect intermediary between heaven and earth. Being extremely good is their great quality. They have a head start, having practiced spiritual methods for the good of humanity in many other incarnations. They can adapt to any environment or situation with ease, speed and without any major security concerns. Their weakness is their critical intelligence, which is symbolic and orderly and makes it difficult for them to choose their ideal partner. People born under this angel's influence will have no worries about diseases, believing in the maxim "healthy mind in healthy body", and if they happen to get ill, they usually end up curing themselves.

Professionally: Anyone born under Anauel's influence might be an anthropologist or palaeontologist and will be able to perform transformations in history, become detached in the study of esoteric philosophies or writings about the life of Christ. Due to their wit, dedication and adaptability, they can succeed in any career they embrace.

Contrary Angel: Dominates madness, decadence and indebtedness. Someone under this influence can become corrupt, borrow money perpetually, ruin themselves due to their misconduct or discover the weakness of people with their sensory faculties and exploit them with an air of arrogance.

Hierarchy: Archangels
Archangel: Michael
Planet: Mercury
Power number: 13
Month of Change: April
Is present on Earth: from 20:40pm to 21:00pm
Incense: Eucalyptus
Colour of Candle: Blue
Weekday: Tuesday
Crystal: Coral
Psalm: 2, verse 10

"Now therefore be wise, you kings. Be instructed, you judges of the earth."

ANGEL OF HUMANITY
Protects days: 05/01 - 19/03 - 31/05 - 12/08 - 24/10

This hierarchy of Angels is called the "Lords of Sacrifice." The energy used for this hierarchy is the power of the word: language. They were so named because in other lives they had a higher level of awareness for the community in which they lived. According to Helena Blavatsky, these beings would be pillars of light, the divine principle that is installed in human form.

"People who are in born on the above days might be wondering "So do I not have a guardian angel?" At first the answer is no, because you already have a very strong angelic essence here on earth due to perfroming humanitarian acts in a previous lifetime in which their life was dedicated to benefit those less fortunate. Due to their soul achievement, as a reward they have been granted permission to be their own Guardian Angel if they so wish" ?

Only the physical presence of people born on 05/01, 19/03, 31/05, 12/08, and 24/10 can ward off the contrary angel opposed to a family or a group. On a cosmic level, they produce the full force of conscience, giving a smart combination, which somehow represents a covenant with God. The friendship or even the union of two people born in the days ruled by the angels of humanity is a divine covenant with God.

The angels of humanity have admirable customs and laws. They must learn to vibrate positively, to have more courage and not to conform to the current opinions of the masses. They must also learn to be enemies of impurity, ignorance and debauchery, to have respect for human beings and honour their words. These immortal souls lived for many centuries. [15:05:37 | Edited 15:05:58] Marcus : Matthews: does it mean this "Humans - even those being their own guardian angel - can never transgress the laws followed here on earth, letting anyone be overenthusiastic using their angelic elements, as higher spiritual laws are in place . If this occurs, their mission is not fulfilled and everything will turn against them.

ANIEL

Invoke this angel to achieve victory and have a decent life. Aniel promotes the study of science and art, makes revelations about the secrets of nature and inspires philosophers during their meditations or lectures.

Influence: Those born under the influence of this angel will become celebrities who will be distinguished by their talents and their messages of positivity – their enthusiasm is overflowing. Sometimes they may become satirical, revolutionary or have crazy ideas, but everything that is shared with the general public will be dignified. They only accept a job offer or a better social status if it is not contrary to their spiritual inspiration. A strong sense of self-control will prevent them from yielding to the temptation of accommodating others unecessarily. Their visions and thoughts of a better world are achieved through prayer or meditation. People born under Aniel's protection will be favoured by those who have a guardian angel of the same class. They will have a small circle of friends who are constant and faithful. They have the possibility of marrying young, often choosing older people. They will fight for the welfare of children and get sad when they do not use the opportunities offered to them. Someone under this angel's influence will have much luck and enjoy many privileges, obtaining good results in competitions, literary and public disputes.

Professionally: Anyone born under Aniel's influence can succeed as a comedian, actor or in any activity relating to the media.

Contrary Angel: Masters of perversity, cheating, materialism, harshness and hardness. Someone dominated by this contrary angel may want to get ahead in life at any cost, make false claims or neglect the welfare of the family.

Hierarchy: Powers
Archangel: Camael
Planet: Moon
Power number: 11
Month of Change: November
Is present on Earth: from 12:05pm to 12:20pm
Incense: Chamomile
Colour of Candle: Dark Yellow
Weekday: Thursday
Crystal: Tiger Eye
Psalm: 79, verse 9

"Help us, God of our salvation, for the glory of your name. Deliver us, and forgive our sins, for your name's sake."

ARIEL
Protects days: 20/02 - 04/05 - 16/07 - 27/09 - 09/12

Invoke this angel to help you thank God, who sends blessings and gifts. Ariel facilitates the discovery of hidden treasures, reveals the secrets of nature through dreams and can help you find objects that disappear outside of your home.

Influence: Those born under the influence of this angel will have a subtle and strong spirit, good ideas and sublime thoughts. They will be discreet, act prudently, make decisions at the right time and manage to solve the most difficult problems. They will enjoy meditating and understanding the secrets of the mystical and occult - discoveries that will benefit the purification of the spirit. People under Ariel's protection will work in the service of spirituality in favour of their peers. They will use technological means such as computer science, dowsing equipment, trans-communication aura-meters and similar techniques and equipment to feel the frequency or the permanence of the enchanted. The entire angelic world is at your disposal thanks to their work on Earth. Someone born under this angel's influence represents power, achievement and proof that the harmony of man with God is essential to wellbeing. All aspects of their life are predisposed to triumph. They will occupy a prominent place in society and engage with the problems of people who seek and find the right path with wisdom. They will never lack respect for the older or more experienced.

Their motto is "all forms of communication are meant to be". They do not allow people to appeal to the instinct or irrational. Their reasoning allows for an astral crown of gold to be bestowed upon them, which means the ownership of intellectual light.

Professionally: Those born under Ariel's influence can be successful in any activity related to human resources. Their interest in the study of minerals, crystals and especially botany will open the way for activities in these areas. They can live and work in the world of arts for its beauty and charm.

Contrary Angel: Masters failure, indecision, immaturity, theft and scandal. A person dominated by this contrary angel may be weak-minded, reckless and lead a spiritual life plagued by troubles.

Hierarchy: Virtues
Archangel: Raphael
Planet: Saturn
Power number: 14
Month of Change: May
Is present on Earth: from 15:00pm to 15:20pm
Incense: Sandalwood
Colour of Candle: White
Weekday: Thursday
Crystal: Topaz
Psalm: 144, verse 9

"I will sing a new song to you, God. On a ten-stringed lyre, I will sing praises to you."

ASALIAH

Protects days: 21/02 - 05/05 – 07/17 - 28/09 - 10/12

Invoke this angel to help you have knowledge of the Laws of God, to raise awareness to help uncover the truth in the process and to achieve constructive goals. Asaliah facilitates the understanding of how to contemplate the divine represented in nature.

Influence: Those born under the influence of this angel will be builders of angelic plans, sweet and tender by nature, with a pleasant character and able to stand out because of their enormous charisma. They will be fair and incorruptible in faith. The truth will be a constant in their attitudes. People under Asaliah's protection will be dynamic, living their day-to-day life in a spectacular fashion and taking advantage of every second to the immediate realisation of every idea that comes up. They can go beyond their own forces without dissipating energy. Sleek and strong, their hands are always ready to act immediately, with skill and mastery. Those born under this angel's influence will be able to make sacrifices and strongly pursue their ideals, even when conditions seem unfavourable. They will be virtuous, sensitive and stubborn. Their aura of wisdom will be found in the frontal region, with a sign in the third eye between the eyebrows. They do not like confusion, especially of a sentimental nature. Their taste maybe noticeable in their well-furnished and comfortable home and their clothes will be of good quality too. People under Asaliah's protection are proud without being snobbish and sincerely accept the doctrines of others. They will always be transforming the way whilst preserving the essence of God.

Professionally: Those born under this angels influence maybe successful as entrepreneurs, designers or surgeons or in any activity where the firmness and dexterity of hands is important. They will find it easy to express themselves and maybe great orators or teachers.

Contrary Angel: Masters scandalous and immoral actions, public scandals and dangerous systems. A person dominated by this angel might spread untrue rumours, be permissive, engage in multiple love affairs, and commit sexual crimes or violence in the act of love.

Hierarchy: Virtues
Archangel: Raphael
Planet: Venus
Power number: 10
Month of Change: October
Is present on Earth: from 15:20pm to 15:40pm
Incense: Jasmine
Colour of Candle: White
Weekday: Friday
Crystal: Pink Tourmoline
Psalm: 104, verse 24

"O LORD, how manifold are thy works! In wisdom hast thou made them all: the earth is full of thy riches."

AYEL

Protects days: 13/03 - 25/05 - 06/08 - 18/10 - 30/12

Invoke this angel to help bring comfort against adversity or injustice. Ayel promotes longevity as well as preservation and consolidation of material goods purchased through labour. This angel influences studies, especially philosophy, mysticism or religion. Ayel also masters change.

Influence: Those born under this angels influence are, illuminated by the spirit of God. They will be sound in enterprise, especially in studies and research of high esoteric sciences. Influential and reliable, they will not endorse the views of duplicity or dishonesty. They will transform all dreams and projects into achievements, since nothing exceeds the limit of their possibilities. Averse to futility, they will always be happy with themselves and not interested in anything other than demonstrations of affection, knowing that they are absolutely sincere. Someone born under Ayel's protection will devote all their attention to the family and is always there to help others reach their goals with deserved success. Their health enhanced because they never give in to excesses, understanding that the body is the temple of the soul. Their back is well protected against instability or misunderstanding of their actions. They can move forward with confidence as their guardian angel will always be by their side.

Professionally: Someone born under this angel's influence is always assuming new roles and getting more tasks done, which makes them happier as well as highly recognised and remunerated for it. They are successful in their jobs, especially in trade.

Contrary Angel: Masters envy, bitterness, gluttony, error and bias. A person dominated by this contrary angel might be a charlatan or an author or writer, with the tendency to create agenda's to their advantage. They may harm others, cause frustration or nostalgia of the past or like cheap seduction, even in daily family and professional life.

Hierarchy: Angels
Archangel: Gabriel
Planet: Saturn
Power number: 4
Month of Change: April
Is present on Earth: from 22:00 to 22:20
Incense: Chamomile
Colour of Candle: White
Weekday: Wednesday
Crystal: White Quartz
Psalm: 36, verse 5

"Thy mercy, O LORD, is in the heavens; and thy faithfulness reached unto the clouds."

CAHETHEL
Protects days: 01/13 - 03/27 - 06/08 - 8/20 - 01/11

Invoke this angel for protection by God and to inspire man to thank God for produce from the land. This angel has control over agricultural production, especially in areas that are necessary for the survival of humans and animals.

Influence: Those born under this angels influence have harmony and balance between spirit and matter as well as maturity and mastery over themselves. They have a clear vision and understanding of the world and its laws, and always keep moving forward. Due to their spiritual maturity, they often feel out of place among friends or relatives, who have difficulty understanding them. They follow their heart, have great intuition and are humble when they speak their knowledge with wisdom and understanding. They are not afraid of anything and are always ready - suitcases packed - to travel and discover new horizons. Someone born under Cahethel's protection might be a pioneer in agricultural production. Using modern methods 'and advanced technology'. Their land is their life and their home. They share their prosperity generously with their closest friends and family. Although their success can be attributed to luck, they are always grateful to God for everything they receive.

Professionally: People born under the influence of this angel, can succeed in agronomy or veterinary medicine, especially in the field of animal reproduction. They can become wealthy landowners or merchants of agricultural products and enjoy growing herbs, flowers and fruit trees. Someone born under Cahethel's protection can be dedicated to landscaping or become an expert in medicinal plants. They may be very curious about Bach Flowers or making perfumes with floral fragrances. They can succeed with anything that has to do with land or nature, because they respect and uphold its laws.

Contrary Angel: Dominates pride, blasphemy, atheism and corruption. A person dominated by this contrary angel may do everything that is harmful to agricultural production: produce only for their own profit and in their interest, never share, speculate for immediate profit, sell infertile land, burn everything or produce noxious plants such as the poppy or others which are harmful hallucinogens. They may cause conflicting situations with family or behave as though they were above the law, especially those of nature. By acting this way, their activities always have mediocre results.

Hierarchy: Seraphim
Archangel: Metraton
Planet: Saturn
Power number: 6
Month of Change: June
Is present on Earth: from 2:20am to 2:40am
Incense: Peppermint
Colour of Candle: White
Weekday: Wednesday
Crystal: Moon Stone
Psalm: 94, verse 22

"But the LORD is my defense; and my God is the rock of my refuge."

CALIEL

Protects days: 23/01 - 06/04 - 06/18 - 30/08 - 11/11

Invoke this angel to help against adversity, for the triumph of the innocent who are confused by evil (negative energies and spirits) and to know the truth in the process.

Influence: Those born under Caliel's influence are intelligent and charismatic, have great wit, a strong personal magnetism as well as enormous patience and perseverance. They look with love upon every little manifestation in everyday life. They are great light workers who can perform miracles, because their faith is unshakable. People under this angel's protection are incorruptible and love justice, truth and integrity. They have extraordinary intuition when it comes to uncovering the truth and the ability to identify true intention with just one look. They can analyse any situation calmly and objectively and their logic is unassailable. They do not like things to be vague or abstract; they always want to understand everything in every detail.

Professionally: Those born under angel Caliel's influence can succeed as journalists, writers or lawyers, or in any activities relating to the judiciary.

Contrary Angel: Masters intrigue, black magic, perversity and a taste for scandal. A person dominated by this contrary angel may have a tendency to lie or be the author of anonymous letters or writings of slanderous or libellous comments. For them, justice may be a pretext for expressions of anger or revenge. They may engage in scandalous cases just to meet dignitaries.

Hierarchy: Thrones
Archangel: Tsaphkiel
Planet: Mercury
Power number: 10
Month of Change: October
Is present on Earth: from 5:40am to 6:00am
Incense: Peppermint
Colour of Candle: Baby Blue
Weekday: Monday
Crystal: Turquise
Psalm: 7, verse 9

"Oh let the wickedness of the wicked come to an end; but establish the just for the righteous God trieth the hearts and reins."

CHAVAKIAH

Protects days: 09/02 - 23/04 - 05/07 - 16/09 - 28/11

Invoke this angel to be at peace with everyone, to eliminate negative energies of people who want to hurt you or to assist in the reconciliation process of spouses. Chavakiah will help maintain peace and harmony among families. This angel also governs over wills, inheritance and matters of estate.

Influence: Those born under Chavakiah's influence will be major contributors to social welfare, often at the cost or even sacrifice of their personal interests. They love to live in peace with everyone and see people reconciled. They are practically minded with the ability to make wise decisions. Their morality is always under tight control and they may even suppress their feelings. Always attentive to detail, they will speak in a pleasant and mindful way, never using force, to make themselves understood. Their emotional wellbeing will depend on approval of others in their social life. They will probably be physically attractive and not too worried about finding their soul mate. People born under Chavakiah's protection have an immense dislike of extravagant attitudes or social scandals. Their daily work will be arduous and full of character. They should avoid being too austere and demanding of themselves. Wealth will help them promote issues related to medicine and spirituality.

Professionally: Anyone born under this angel's influence will flourish in careers in public relations or sociology. They may work on projects to solve problems related to ecology or education. They will develop their gift of telepathic communication, which can help in their work.

Contrary Angel: Masters of debauchery, dislike, discrimination and confusion. A person dominated by this contrary angel may become involved in unfair legal proceedings, harmful situations, evil moral judgments or they may treat employees like slaves.

Hierarchy: Powers
Archangel: Camael
Planet: Mercury
Power number: 6
Month of Change: June
Is present on Earth: from 11:20am to 11:40am
Incense: Benjoim or Myrh
Colour of Candle: White
Weekday: Sunday
Crystal: Jaspe
Psalm: 114, verse 1

"When Israel went out of Egypt, the house of Jacob from a people of strange language; Judah was his sanctuary, and Israel his dominion."

DAMABIAH
Protects days: 11/3 - 23/05 - 04/08 - 16/10 - 28/12

Invoke this angel to protect against spells and negative omens, or to help acquire victory and positive results. Damabiah favours sailors, pilots, those who work in coastal towns or undertake maritime expeditions for research, and all kinds of maritime trade related activities.

Influence: Those born under this angel's influence will have a considerable fortune and be exalted where they live, enjoying prosperity in their local community. They are called adventurous, since they live life in profound ways, which attains the grace of their guardian angel. They believe they can only improve themselves in life by experiencing wholeness. They are generous and noble, have a very enlightened spirit and will have a huge chance of success. Anyone under Damabiah's protection will love all that is mystical and esoteric and will strive to combat envy. They will have financial help for their research, which can become historical, or to organise major events that have an impact on society. They will be constantly moving, without much planning and without any problem in leaving everything behind. Someone born under this angel's influence is a person of the world, who will not waste energy unnecessarily and show that by searching for enlightenment and wisdom we can overcome misfortune. They are always respected, by legions of people, who they can positively influence with their experience, by relating their success story. People born under Damabiah's protection will always embrace matters of the heart. They love their freedom and will reject any relationship that makes them feel imprisoned. Faithful to their ideals, they will never make anyone suffer for their own selfishness or attempt to take advantage of a defenceless person. They are servants of God!

Hierarchy: Angels
Archangel: Gabriel
Planet: Moon
Power number: 7
Month of Change: July
Is present on Earth: from 21:20pm to 21:40pm
Incense: Eucaliptus
Colour of Candle: Light Blue
Weekday: Saturday
Crystal: Hematite
Psalm: 89, verse 13

"Thou hast a mighty arm: strong is thy hand, and high is thy right hand."

DANIEL
Protects days: 24/02 - 05/05 - 20/07 - 01/10 - 13/12

Invoke this angel to help obtain God's mercy and have consolation. Angel Daniel promotes justice, the clergy and magistracy. He gives inspiration to not be hesitant or embarrassed.

Influence: Those born under the influence of Angel Daniel will work and perform all activities with much love. This angel will bring luck and protection against diseases. Notice that your intuition can reach genius when invited to debates or when you are among friends. Those born under Daniel's influence are determined, fair, patient to the extreme and able to support almost all people. They dislike anything that is unclear or not well explained and do not accept being unjustly reproached – they may be tough and aggressive if the person is not right. They must think before taking action, not feel threatened and risk turning dreams into impossible fantasies. They are motivators and public people, able to handle any issue, discover the "why" of many social problems and convince society that their proposals are satisfactory to become successful. In childhood they may have had problems in showing affection to parents, so it will be common to see those under this influence fussing over children, probably to compensate for this deficiency. This angel can be invoked to work with more sweetness, warmth and balance when they find an environment like their home.

Some events in adolescence may mark their life, giving them full assurance that the guardian angel is always there protecting and keeping them safe through their intelligence and interior connection to the astral world.

Professionally: Those born under this angels influence adapt very well in activities related to foreign trade or international companies. With their eloquence they may be great orators, succeed in politics or acting.

Contrary Angel: Dominates blackmail, anguish, frustration, physical and verbal aggression with parents. A person born under the influence of this angel may create barriers in industry, to be skilled at spinning intrigues, a hustler or con man who enjoys working and living by illegal means.

Hierarchy: Principalities
Archangel: Haniel
Planet: Moon
Power number: 5
Month of Change: May
Is present on Earth: from 16:20pm to 16:40pm
Incense: Peppermint
Colour of Candle: White or Silver
Weekday: Wednesday
Crystal: Ruby
Psalm: 102, verse 8

"Mine enemies reproach me all the day, and they that are mad against me are sworn against me."

ELEMIAH

Protects days: 09/01 - 03/23 - 06/04 - 08/16 - 28/10

Invoke this angel when the spirit is tormented, or if you need to reconsider the facts. Elemiah is a source of wisdom and helps resolve psychological problems. This angel also assists with travel and sea expeditions, also influences useful discoveries and helps recognise traitors.

Influence: Those born under this angel's protection have divine potential. They are certain to discover their potential at a very early stage. They love to open people's minds with ideas and new proposals. Sometimes they are sad, because even people they consider friends, envy their good fortune. Deep in their heart they feel a strong urge to help people, especially the most deprived. They don't often give alms to the poor, but never refuse to aid those who genuinely wish to improve their lives through work. Anyone born under Elemiah's influence has a strong potential to heal others. Endowed with great luck and charisma, they are always considered the best at what they do. They always have a strong gut feeling when something happens. Having a strong intuition helps them in their life. Explanations for problems in their life enter their unconscious mind, without the need to seek external guidance to resolve these problems. Those born under this angel's influence will find fundamental philosophies in their lifestyle. It would be interesting for them to know their genealogical tree, as they could perhaps find a distant relative, whose exploits could be recorded historically. Anyone under Elemiah's protection is, predisposed to rebuild their life based on knowledge of primitive societies. They will probably like archaeology, anthropology or etymology. They are always working on several projects simultaneously.

Professionally: Those born under the influence of this angel can perform activities related to crude oil, mining and other minerals. They have the capability to explore creative avenues and maybe invited to create new companies with high technology. They can also work as police or security officers with great competence. Every person born under Elemiah's protection is on earth to make changes, yet always with humility and with their feet on the ground.

Contrary Angel: Influences discoveries dangerous to society, poor education, passivity with regards to violence, sadism and sexual perversion. A person who lets themselves be dominated by this contrary angel maybe interested and curious about toxins and hallucinogens. They can cause hindrances or barriers to business or restrict commerce or industry.

Hierarchy: Seraphim
Archangel: Metatron
Planet: Mercury
Power number: 11
Month of Change: November
Is present on Earth: from 1:00am to 1:20am
Incense: Sandalwood
Colour of Candle: Light Yellow
Weekday: Wednesday
Crystal: Tiger Eye

Psalm: 6, verse 5

"For in death there is no remembrance of thee: in the grave who shall give thee thanks?"

HAAIAH
Protects days: 31/01 - 14/04 - 06/26 - 07/09 - 19/11

Invoke this angel to help you win or make processes and judgments favourable to their cause. Haaiah can also be invoked to help man contemplate things and acts of God. This angel dominates politicians, diplomats, ambassadors and influences journalists.

Influence: Those born under Haaiah's protection are just and benevolent and have appreciation for logical solutions. They like serious relationships, are endowed with compassion and balance. They know that earthly laws can and should be changed. They respect the laws of the universe, as these can never be violated. People under this angel's influence, tend to use special vinculum when communicating with others as a synonym for change and renewal. They work tirelessly in search of knowledge to build their ideals. They like to travel and adapt easily to climate, people and language. Thanks to their outstanding personality and beauty of character, they have access to the highest spheres of society and government. As messengers of peace, they will be conscious collaborators well aware of divine providence, with a transcendental mission. Establishing the divine order, they will be spiritual mentors (even without being aware of it, because their spirit has ascended).

Professionally: Those born, under influence of, Haaiah can be successful working with oracles or as a tour guide, pilot or politician.

Contrary Angel: Masters of ambition, conspiracy, betrayal, black magic and indiscretion. A person dominated by this contrary angel will not know how to keep secrets, oppose just causes, violate mail or mistreat people who want to help.

Hierarchy: Domination
Archangel: Uriel
Planet: Moon
Power number: 4
Month of Change: April
Is present on Earth: from 8:20am to 8:40am
Incense: Fennel
Colour of Candle: White
Weekday: Saturday
Crystal: Moonstone
Psalm: 118, verse 16

"The right hand of the LORD is exalted: the right hand of the Lord Doeth valiantly."

HAAMIAH

Protects days: 01/12 - 12/02 - 26/04 - 08/07 - 19/09

Haamiah corresponds to the holy name of God – Agla, which means God in Trinity with the One. What matters is that this divine name helps to discover all the treasures and secrets of the Earth, reciting verse 9 of psalm 90 (89 of the Christian Bible). Cabalists say that this psalm protects against the spirits of ignorant primitives.

Influence: Those born under angel Haamiah's influence serve God because of their great intelligence and awareness gained through their studies. Their wisdom is, used by God to unify all religions of the world; so they will then be called Universalists. They will be sympathetic to the problems of the world and manage to solve them using their prodigious intuition. Anyone under this angel's protection will passionately, defend, individual freedoms and fight against prejudice. They will fight with all their strength against evil people who use dark magic and defend God with the most powerful weapon - the truth. Their mission on earth will be to elevate humankind to ascension. They will have a great facility to accept things that other people find surprising or unintelligible. People born, under the influence of Haamiah will prove their own pattern for love, rejecting convention. They feel attracted to eccentric people and hate scenes of jealousy and possessiveness. They dislike being rushed to change pre-established plans.

Professionally: Those born under this angel's protection feel a strong calling for the esoteric. They will be great legislators of divine science or great healers and possess splendid culture. They will show the truth with great magnitude through rites, celebrations or in their daily work. Their mind, which goes beyond frontiers, will be able to do scientific research. If they have opportunities to study; they will be celebrated for their discoveries in technology or nuclear science. Otherwise they will use their powers of clairvoyance and telepathy to penetrate the frontiers of the spiritual world.

Contrary Angel: Calls to error, lies, fanaticism and irritation. A person dominated by this contrary angel may act against all moral or religious principles, make sacrilegious paintings, be inflexible, not accept criticism and judge alone against any topic.

Hierarchy: Powers
Archangel: Camael
Planet: Saturn
Power number: 4
Month of Change: April
Is present on Earth: from 12:20am to 12:40am
Incense: Fennel
Colour of Candle: Yellow
Weekday: Monday
Crystal: Amber
Psalm: 90, verse 9

"For all our days are passed away in thy wrath: we spend our years as a tale that is told."

HABUHIAH
Protects days: 14/03 - 26/05 - 07/08 - 19/10 - 31/12

Invoke this angel to help preserve peace, eliminate the power of evil and cure health problems. Habuhiah influences agriculture, breeding and fertility.

Influence: Those born under this angel's influence have class and elegance. They are noble and selfless in relationships due to their dominating spirit-instinct. Their good mood is contagious. They are powerful, intelligent and have a deep analytical capacity. They can catalogue everything that comes to hand, letting go of what is not of interest, no matter what. People, under the influence of Habuhiah will behave honestly, which will be a protection against weaknesses and negative influences. They often think "the door is closed", but they should know that for every closed door their angel will open many more. God will deliver your future with confidence and security. In order for them to progress on their path, it is important that they use their ability amongst their loved ones, making sure they don't leave any sorrow or bitterness behind. Equipped with protection from the elements, especially those related to land, they might have the need to stay in touch with their guardian angel, so that their intelligence can manifest and produce great ideas.

Professionally: Someone born under Habuhiah's influence can work in any activity relating to nature. They will have great ability with their hands, especially at planting (agriculture or gardens), exploring aromas, herbs and plants, including their history. They could be great herbalists, agronomists, gardeners, botanists or work with Bach flowers.

Contrary Angel: Masters presumption, sterility and hunger. A person dominated by this contrary angel may want bad luck for the family, have a critical attitude against those who have the ability to teach or facilitate the spread of diseases like AIDS.

Hierarchy: Angels
Archangel: Gabriel
Planet: Moon
Power number: 10
Month of Change: October
Is present on Earth: from 22:20pm to 22:40pm
Incense: Sandalwood and Lavander
Colour of Candle: Green
Weekday: Friday
Crystal: Green Quartz
Psalm: 105, verse 7

"He is the LORD our God: his judgments are in all the earth."

HAHAHEL
Protects days: 15/02 - 29/04 - 11/07 - 22/09 - 04/12

Invoke this angel against detractors or enemies of religion. Hahahel protects the true word of Jesus, his missionaries and individuals who get involved in ministry to obtain peace.

Influence: Those born under this angel's influence love truth are dutiful and fulfil their obligations. They have strong powers of concentration and the wisdom to discern and judge. They face issues with maturity in their hearts. Someone born under Hahahel's protection will always act in harmony with the laws of the universe. They feel to a great depth that God has reserved a great mission for them. But where do they start? Most likely, by finding the right partner worthy of good ideas and with a noble character, because their mission is to be accompanied by their soul partner. They will want to have children, so these children can continue teaching truth. Hahahel grants the gift of communication, charisma and the ability to learn from various subjects, mainly connected to the esoteric. A person born under the influence of this angel will probably begin their spiritual work at an early age, dedicated to serving God and seeking the truth. They will teach people how to enter a new path in their lives, one that transcends temples and which comes from the heart. They may have views that conflict with other religions, as they tend to be spiritual, and do not follow any particular religion. Experts in many religious dialects, they will study in a rational way and be specialists in deciphering sacred writings. People under Hahahel's protection will have many friends and supporters of their ideas. They will put immense energy into serving the common good and are transformers of the world. They will be blessed with much luck, a wonderful life and be very happy.

Professionally: Anyone born under the influence of this angel can be successful as a doctor, nurse, social worker, psychologist, sociologist or teacher, or in any activity related to esotericism. Their vocation will probably be found in areas related to religion, spirituality, esotericism or metaphysics. They might be great missionaries, inside or outside a religious order.

Contrary Angel: Masters dishonour, worship of idols, necromancy, profane rituals and ceremonies or erotic scandal. A person dominated by this contrary angel may act with social misconduct where they live. They may have contempt for the meek and those who have difficulty learning. They may be false prophets and use their knowledge erroneously, only to benefit from material gain.

Hierarchy: Virtues
Archangel: Raphael
Planet: Jupiter
Power number: 10
Month of Change: October
Is present on Earth: from 13:20pm to 13:40pm
Incense: Sandalwood and Lavander
Colour of Candle: White
Weekday: Thursday
Crystal: Turquoise

Psalm: 119, verse 2

"Blessed are they that keep his testimonies and that seek him with the whole heart."

HAHAHIAH
Protects days: 17/01 - 03/31 - 06/12 - 24/08 - 05/11

This angel takes a strong stance against opponents and brings revelations, especially in dreams, regarding hidden mysteries.

Influence: Those born under this angel's influence have a strong personality, intelligence, spirituality and discretion. Their face is pleasant, their manner is gentle. S/he is serene, cordial and acts with moderation and balance, has great inner happiness and understands the world and people easily. They will faithfully follow the teachings of this angel, studying all the information that is passed in stages, and are very didactic and thorough. Their mission will be to ensure that people study and achieve knowledge through books. They will have strong brotherly feelings and have a special gift for the caring of people abandoned in nursing homes and hospices. Always offering good advice they will be experts at calming people who are nervous. They will always act according to the law and will be a living example through their deeds that always work. His/her inner voice is synchronized with the laws of the universe. They will succeed in the esoteric world, because the light is a natural thing in their life. They have appreciation for the esoteric sciences, especially the Eastern. They will naturally see the auras of people, without knowing how it works, spontaneously and full of peace. His/her relationship with the opposite sex will be easy, due to their lush beauty and tremendous charisma.

Professionally: likely to achieve success in activities related to medicine and psychology and they may be the author of psychological treatises. As a hobby, they may be involved with something connected to the manufacture of cosmetics, prosthetics, or objects designed to improve the appearance of people with physical defects.

Contrary Angel: Masters indiscretion, inadequacy, delinquency and sexual availability. A person under the influence of this angel can use hallucinogens as a means to achieve spiritual ecstasy. They can abuse the trust of people, mostly women, molesting them sexually. Their refinement is lying to lure their victims.

Hierarchy: Cherubim
Archangel: Raphael
Planet: Neptune
Power number: 5
Month of Change: May
Is present on Earth: from 13:20pmto 13:40pm
Incense: Rosemary and Lavander
Colour of Candle: Lilac
Weekday: Sunday
Crystal: Pearl
Psalm: 9, verse 18

"For the needy shall not always be forgotten: the expectation of the poor shall not perish for ever."

HAHASIAH
Protects days: 25/02 - 09/05 - 21/07 - 02/10 - 14/12

Invoke this angel to help elevate the soul to God, to contemplate the divine and discover all the mysteries through consciousness and intelligence.

Influence: Those born under the influence of Hahasiah will love all sciences and feel a special interest in knowing the properties and attributes of animals, plants and minerals. They will be neat, creative and lead their life in harmony due to the immense light protection that is in their heart. Studious, they will learn the ways of using keen intuition and understanding the divine order in human structures. As spiritual mentors, as masters and experts of the esoteric sciences they will gain prestige and authority to teach courses or give lectures. Anyone under this angel's protection will work to find peace between people. They know that when they go through difficulty, it is nothing more than a means to access internal and external divinity. They are lovers of nature, with simple tastes and always aware of fine detail. They may enjoy romanticism, painting, music, perfumes or similar pleasures. Their poetic side flows easily. A letter or drawing of a simple heart could be the sublime manifestation of their guardian angel. People born under Hahasiah's influence will have many revelations and give importance to the beginning of their spiritual teachings. Their conscience will be their own "Temple of Mystery". They will be their own priest, thus building the realisation of the truth of God on earth.

Professionally: A person born under the influence of this angel can excel in medicine, research and wonderful inventions for the benefit of mankind. They have ability in abstract sciences and a talent for any activity relating to biological sciences.

Contrary Angel: Masters of charlatans and black magic. Someone dominated by this contrary angel may abuse the good faith of people, promising extraordinary things that cannot be achieved or use objects to convince customers of their power. They might not be able to contain their impulses or satisfy their sexuality. They may not be physically clean or live like a beggar.

Hierarchy: Principalities
Archangel: Haniel
Planet: Moon
Power number: 10
Month of Change: October
Is present on Earth: from 16:40pm to 17:00pm
Incense: Peppermint/Mint
Colour of Candle: White
Weekday: Monday
Crystal: Pearl
Psalm: 103, verse 21

"Bless ye the LORD, all ye his hosts; ye ministers of his that do his pleasure."

HAHEUIAH
Protects days: 29/01 - 12/04 - 24/06 - 05/09 - 17/11

Invoke this angel to obtain the grace and mercy of God.

Influence: Those born under the influence of this angel, tend to live with their family for a long period and often even after marriage, seek to reside in nearby buildings, living almost every day with their families. Endowed with great spiritual power, maturity and insight, they will be a great friend, whom everyone likes. They are intelligent and analytical, and will seek answers within religious concepts, for everything that goes on in the world. They have great concern for the safety, both in the family, and within a group or community.

Professionally: Those born under this angel's influence maybe successful as a politician, lawyer or human rights defender or any activity related to sciences and security. Connoisseur of the arts, loves studying and enjoy reading as a hobby.

Contrary Angel: Masters dominance, violence, kidnapping and terrorism. A person dominated by the influence of this genius, may, through his writings, incite people to violence. May protect delinquents and do crimes in the name of religion or spirituality, making use of "entities".

Hierarchy: Thrones
Archangel: Tsaphkiel

Planet: Venus
Power number: 4
Month of Change: April
Is present on Earth: from 07:40pm to 08:00pm
Incense: Sandalwood
Colour of Candle: Green
Weekday: Monday
Crystal: Blue Topaz
Psalm: 32, verse 5

"I acknowledged my sin unto thee, and mine iniquity have I not hid. I said, I will confess my transgressions unto the LORD; and thou forgives the iniquity of my sin."

HAIAIEL

Protects days: 17/03 - 29/05 - 10/08 - 22/10 - 03/01

Invoke this angel to help confuse negative people or release links with people who want to oppress us. Haiaiel protects all who use the light of truth. This angel dominates victory and peace. Haiaiel helps people have strength, energy, talent and more confidence in all activities.

Influence: Those born under the influence of this angel have strength to fight against any injustice and know to discern between right and wrong. They combat falsehood and will be known for the way they express themselves. Their way of thinking, essentially correct, is reflected in their behaviour. Their work pace is fast and they tend to be ahead of schedule. A person born under Haiaiel's protection feels safe with the support of their spouse and family, which will never be a source of problems. Loyal and worried about their private life, they need moments of stillness and isolation, although they don't enjoy living alone because it makes them anxious. They must remember that all the hard times lead to spiritual growth. Their existence is synonymous with abundance and happiness.

Professionally: Anyone born under this angel's influence will have success when involved in litigation, financial transactions or estate dealings. Any kind of financial speculation will bring those advantages. They find it easy to work in crafts such as woodwork or sculpture, which can be a hobby.

Contrary Angel: Masters greed, unnecessary debt, waste, corruption, discord, envy, cheating, unhappy marriage and sloth. A person dominated by this contrary angel might be a bad investment advisor or become famous for their crimes.

Hierarchy: Angels
Archangel: Gabriel
Planet: Mars
Power number: 11
Month of Change: November
Is present on Earth: from 23:20pm to 23:40pm
Incense: Rosemary
Colour of Candle: White
Weekday: Tuesday
Crystal: White Quartz
Psalm: 108, verse 3

"I will praise thee, O LORD, among the people: and I will sing praises unto thee among the nations."

HARAHEL
Protects days: 05/03 - 17/05 - 29/07 - 10/10 - 22/12

Invoke this angel to help cure problems in the reproductive organs, especially of women, and to promote a long life without health problems. Harahel makes children obedient and respectful to parents, relatives, teachers and fellow students. This angel favours stockbrokers, brokerage agents, people who work in public agencies, archives, libraries and those with any collections (especially rare and precious ones).

Influence: Those born under Harahel's influence will be eager to educate themselves, seeking knowledge in all sciences. They are beautiful, possess enormous charisma and will be distinguished by their virtues: nobility of spirit, humour and bravery. Their spirituality is so rich that they will transmit their teachings with patience and dedication, without the pressure of profits. With this gift, if they have a channel to externalise it, they can create paintings, practice healing or work with psychic oracles. Anyone under this angel's protection often earns money in unexpected ways, which will mostly be used for the mission to be fulfilled in their earthly existence. They tend to be mature and have good family relationships, living in harmony with their children. Due to their lust for life, they love exploring the unknown. As great strategists of life, they are always ready to regenerate the personalities of society's misfits. Their refinements will be wonderful and they use the power of their angel to be happy.

Professionally: Those born under the influence of this angel will trade successfully or be great professionals in finance or administration. They can become respected through study or explore innovative ideas in the domain of biology, specialising in breeding plants or animals. They have the possibility of winning scholarships and enhancing their practice and study with their intellectual gifts.

Contrary Angel: Masters fraud, falsification, destruction and ruin. A person dominated by this contrary angel might be the enemy of light, cause fires or destroy with fire, be envious of their neighbour's property, deplete assets that do not belong to them (of family, industry or government) or falsify data to infiltrate computer memory.

Hierarchy: Archangels
Archangel: Michael
Planet: Sun
Power number: 7
Month of Change: July
Is present on Earth: from 19:20pm to 19:40pm
Incense: Lavender
Colour of Candle: Lime Green
Weekday: Saturday
Crystal: Amber
Psalm: 112, verse 3

"Wealth and riches shall be in his house: and his righteousness endured for ever."

HARIEL

Protects days: 20/01 - 03/04 - 15/06 - 27/08 - 08/11

Invoke this angel to help with non-believers (atheists) and to discover all that is useful and new. Hariel protects the sciences and arts. This angel's influence is linked to divine feelings, which are connected with purity.

Influence: Those born under Hariel's influence will have great purity of feeling. Their material and social values will be simple yet refined. Irresistibly perfect, they will tend towards studies of the esoteric sciences, organise associations or promote conferences related to the subject or work to establish the legalisation of esoteric alternatives. They will exalt spirituality and have great enlightenment that happens consciously. They will institute rites and customs that may contribute to the expansion of spirituality. A person under this angel's protection has immense power for prayer and ability to combat materialism to improve human existence. They will hold authority on earth and always find enlightenment to choose the path that they must follow. They have extraordinary analytical intelligence and a strong sense of justice. People born under Hariel's influence are realistic and always have their feet on the ground. They are always humorous, showing that life is very simple without the need for complication. They will have the ability to learn, create and study very quickly. Hariel will require them to do things quickly without wasting time, because the angel works in this fashion.

One year in their life is comparable to five years in the life of any other person.

Professionally: A person born under the influence of this angel can be successful as a lawyer, teacher, scholar, craftsman or restorer of paintings or antiquities.

Contrary Angel: Masters cataclysms and wars of religion. Influences heretics to spread dangerous methods, make the discovery of new dangerous methods or support forms of opposition to esoteric movements. Someone dominated by this contrary angel will be individualistic and selfish. They may call themselves a guru or spiritual guide and form groups to worship themselves. They will be brilliant defenders and propagators of erroneous doctrines and great organisers of religious wars at the international level.

Hierarchy: Cherubim
Archangel: Raziel
Planet: Mars
Power number: 12
Month of Change: December
Is present on Earth: from 4:40am to 5:00am
Incense: Rosemary
Colour of Candle: White
Weekday: Friday
Crystal: Ruby
Psalm: 93, verse 2

"Thy testimonies are very sure: holiness become thine house, O LORD, for ever."

HAZIEL

Protects days: 14/01 – 28/03 - 09/06 – 21/08 – 02/11

Invoke this angel to help you attain the grace of God. Haziel dominates kindness and reconciliation. This angel influences the words given to others and agreements made in earnest. Haziel also facilitates easy financial gains for innocent people.

Influence: Those born under the influence of this angel have the grace and mercy of God, because they know and understand not to judge the mistakes of others. They know that experiences happen, so that each victory on a day-to-day level is to be valued. Always forgiving, even of the most serious offences, they transmute negative karma that may have accumulated into positive karma. They will make a loyal companion and good friend, as nobility of character reigns deep in their heart. They do not have feelings of guilt or ask forgiveness for their money or consumer goods, because everything they have has been achieved by virtue of their work. Money is not a problem in their life - they may even waive fortunes if they would have to give up their ideals. Someone born under Haziel's protection will be favoured on issues related to justice, such as the switching and reduction of a sentence or parole etc. Despite obstacles, they always get a well-deserved triumph over any situation. They also have the protection of older and influential people for their brilliant performance in carrying out important work. In difficult times, they can count on divine providence. Their spirituality is achieved through awareness and their spiritual growth is solid and assured. They will enjoy beauty and the arts and may be protectors of the world of cinema.

Professionally: A person born under the influence of this angel can succeed as a politician, judge, lawyer or writer.

Contrary Angel: Masters anger, arrogance and deception. A person dominated by this contrary angel may trade sexual favours for protection, sell the spiritual sciences or encourage violent demonstrations in society through their writing.

Hierarchy: Cherubim
Archangel: Raziel
Planet: Moon
Power number: 8
Month of Change: August
Is present on Earth: from 02:40am to 03:00am
Incense: Rosemary
Colour of Candle: White
Weekday: Friday
Crystal: Opal
Psalm: 24, verse 7

"Lift up your heads, O ye gates; and be ye lift up, ye everlasting doors; and the King of glory shall come in."

HEKAMIAH
Protects days: 21/01 - 04/04 - 16/06 - 28/08 - 09/11

Invoke this angel to protect people in positions of command. Hekamiah intervenes in issues pertaining to courage and fidelity. This angel helps to fight rogues, achieve victory and liberate the oppressed.

Influence: Those born under Hekamiah's influence have a natural aura of peace. Their sincerity is reflected by the nobility and authority of their personality and prestige. They are loyal, brave, true to their oath, sensitive to issues of honour and have an honest character. Loved by all, they will always be respected for their sensitivity. They enjoy changing everything constantly, such as furniture, paint, decoration or restoration of their home as well as their physical appearance, which they give much care and attention to. Being very sensual, they love to keep images of their loved ones as manifestation of the externalisation of their feelings of the past. They are extremely worried about their family, and children will always be their priority, even if a marriage is over.

Professionally: Someone born under this angel's influence can be successful working in the justice system, legislature, Supreme Court or in activities related to culture for their ease in speaking different languages. They may also follow professions related to finance, financial markets, journalism, public relations, communications or those connected with art, beauty and aesthetics.

Contrary Angel: Masters seduction, infidelity, betrayal and rebellion. A person dominated by this contrary angel will know how to obtain money illegally, for example through buying or selling stolen cars. They may use physical force to make themselves understood, spread dangerous drugs, use anonymous letters or get involved in plots in family life. As a hypnotist or "conscious medium", they may use Eastern practices to ruin what people consider holy or religious.

Hierarchy: Cherubim
Archangel: Raziel
Planet: Mars
Power number: 7
Month of Change: August
Is present on Earth: from 05:00am to 05:20am
Incense: Lavander
Colour of Candle: Baby Blue
Weekday: Tuesday
Crystal: Coral
Psalm: 87, verse 7

"As well the singers as the players on instruments shall be there: all my springs are in thee."

IAH-HEL

Protects days: 08/03 - 20/05 - 01/08 - 13/10 - 25/12

This angel helps you obtain wisdom, aid in the stimulation of bright ideas and pacify the violence of the world. Encourages people to live with integrity and honesty.

Influence: Those born under this angel's influence will love tranquility, nobility of character and strength of attitude. They will faithfully fulfil duties and obligations to themselves, family and community. They will practice various sports and can drop everything if it starts to upset them, have the same attitude when this happens in relation to love. They are spiritually evolved and know to use their energy for their own growth and for the good of humanity. Think more of others than themselves. As a child they demonstrate confidence in their actions and know how to manage their anxieties. Born leaders, they accept leadership roles as they have a strong ability to improvise and appreciate challenges. Tactical, always searching for an instant win in every battle. They will be strong to withstand all the situations that are adverse to their emotional structure and know that the only way to achieve goals is through insistence. They endeavour to have a dignified image, transparent and true. They consider people they met during their numerous trips for business or pleasure "experiences" that enrich their intimate world. They are great teachers who attain victory by being who they are – simply love.

Professionally: Those born under the influence of this angel may be athletes, gym instructors or any other sports or the owners of academy. For their ability for leadership they go into politics, likely to be party leaders or governments. Can also be business administrators, businessmen or economists.

Contrary Angel: Masters and dominates scandalous conduct, depravity, futility, luxury (huge expenditures with jewelry, clothes, often without financial conditions). A person under the influence of this angel will be fickle in relationships, entering into relationships only for the money. Provoke intrigues against couples, inducing them to f with bad advice.

Category: Archangels
Prince: Mikael
Lucky number: 6
Month of change: June
Is present on Earth: from 20:20pm to 20:40pm
Incense: Rosemary and Lavender
Colour of Candle: Pink
Weekday: Saturday
Crystal: Rose Quartz
Psalm: 98, verse 2

"The lord hath made known his salvation: his righteousness hath he openly showed in the sight of the heathen."

IEHUIAH

Protects days: 07/02 - 21/04 - 02/07 - 14/09 - 26/11

Invoke this angel to ascertain the people who aim to harm their fellow human beings through treachery and to destroy the evil designs of the envious. This angel protects the noble and those crowned with light.

Influence: Those born under Iehuiah's influence will be considered architects of the works of God. Defenders of the angelic world, their will is to always strive to defend well. Understanding, sympathetic, loving, always well connected and have the recognition of everyone. They know how to manage their inner world, adapting to reality and not allowing the illusions to stand out. Courageous, they will always fight to develop their higher spiritual tendencies, which are elevated. They are people essentially beneficial to others, bestowing upon them light, through good deeds. They will strive to ensure that people will not be ignorant, helping with teachings or finding financial resources for this good cause. They are faithful friends, they must be cautious in choosing a spouse, because s/he needs a quiet home to always demonstrate a balanced personality. By their very high power of concentration, maturity, common sense, balance and spiritual strength, will be invited to occupy positions of leadership.

Professionally: People born under Iehuiah's influence can be a successful teacher, psychologist, social worker or any activity relating to the sciences.

Contrary Angel: This angel dominates insubordination, intolerance and lack of scruples. A person under the influence of this contrary angel may be obsessed by the conquest of material goods. They will be an insufferable chatterbox and will not inspire confidence for their lack of character.

Hierarchy: Powers
Archangel: Camael
Planet: Moon
Power number: 9
Month of Change: September
Is present on Earth: from 10:40am to 11:00am
Incense: Patcholi
Colour of Candle: Pink
Weekday: Monday
Crystal: Moon Stone
Psalm: 33, verse 12

"Blessed is the nation whose God is the Lord, and the people whom He hath closen for his own inheritance."

IEIAIEL
Protects days: 27/01 - 10/04 - 22/06 - 03/09 - 15/11

Invoke this angel for wealth, fame, diplomacy and trade. Influences travel and discovering new ways or vocations.

Influence: Those born under Ieiaiel's influence will be guided by the principle of change, because they know that nothing is permanent and therefore cannot be wasting time in life. Unique and exotic in thinking and acting, often considered a magician and a fool. They have philanthropic ideals, generous, hate suffering and will always be working for the common good. They need to travel and see the mystery of other countries, uncover blind spots. They will be spiritual mediums with an excellent level of paranormal abilities sought by people believing in their strength, seeking comfort in their predictions or premonitions. They will be comprehensive, diplomatic, with great ability to capture the thinking of people with whom they live to improve their lives. They always spread joy and everyone likes to be by their side.

Professionally: Those born under the influence of this angel can be successful as a teacher, psychologist, actor and activities that help with travelling.

Contrary Angel: Masters racism, piracy, misappropriation and plagiarism. A person under the influence of this contrary angel can exploit and oppress their subjects, living extravagantly at the expense of others.

Hierarchy: Thrones
Archangel: Tasphkiel
Planet: Mercury
Power number: 7
Month of change: July
Is present on Earth: from 07:00am to 07:20am
Incense: Eucalyptus
Weekday: Friday
Colour of Candle: White
Crystal: Agath
Psalm: 120, verse 5

"My soul hath long dwelt with him that hateth peace. I am for peace, but when I speak, they are for war."

IEIALEL

Protects days: 04/03 - 16/05 - 28/07 - 09/10 - 21/12

Invoke this angel to remove sorrow and to shame evil and those who bear false witnesses. Confounds evil, protects especially against the evil eye. Impacts on tradesmen, locksmiths, blacksmiths; and those who deal in iron products.

Influence: Those born under Ieialel's influence will be distinguished by their courage and candour. They will have protection from the planet Venus and the corresponding zodiac signs, (Taurus and Libra). They will be considered a lucid person who decides with clarity of expression in all the complicated or compromising situations. Frank and loving temperament, they have a taste for flowers, ornaments and paintings. Optimistic, loves and defends the truth and ensures that everything takes place in perfect order. They are endowed with great affection and strong sense of aesthetics, strength and appreciation of the value of material goods. They accept their sensuality, attaining serenity, while having the tendency to meet all kinds of pleasures without repressing themselves. They are a little introverted and always control their exhibitionist instincts. They dislike indecision and know every opportunity, not venturing into anything that is not conservative or traditional, thus achieving a material and spiritual balance. Since those under this angel's influence suffer from internal conflict, the solution lies in marriage, their bedrock. Their partner must complete them, so they can feel strong in challenges that they will face or undertake.

Professionally: Those born under Ieialel's influence work easily with decorations, ornaments and general marketing or manufacturing products of iron. They may have a strong militant participation and be an activist against nuclear weapons and will use all arguments to defend their ideas.

Contrary Angel: Dominates the bluff, the concealment, the premeditated murder and horrific murders. A person under this angels influence, maybe dangerous. Smuggler of weapons, plunderer of public assets, also a planner of sophisticated revenge attacks.

Hierarchy: Archangels
Archangel: Michael
Planet: Jupiter
Power number: 9
Month of Change: September
Is present on Earth: from 19:00pm to 19:20pm
Incense: Lavender or Rose
Colour of Candle: Bright Yellow
Weekday: Monday
Crystal: Garnet
Psalm: 6, verse 3

"My soul is in deep anguish. How long, Lord, how long? Turn, Lord, and deliver me, save me because of your unfailing love."

IEIAZEL

Protects days: 14/02 - 28/04 - 10/07 - 21/09 - 03/12

Invoke this angel to protect people who perform activities related to the press and literature. Frees and alleviates individuals from depression and panic disorders.

Influence: Those born under this angels influence, love reading, science and all general knowledge. They will have bright ideas and be prominent in society, being endowed with extreme confidence. They will always be guided by others to assume leadership positions and readily understand the problems experienced by others, unable to say no when they need to; even though some do not deserve their help. They are careless with money, which never fails them. They think that love is worth everything, only marrying for love, hoping that their affection is reciprocated. They will have an imaginative mind, photographic memory and although not accepting of their own mediumship, their conclusions will be drawn more from intuition than by logic. They do a lot of travelling and live in various countries, showing in each place they go, the richness of their personality and the nobility of their character.

Professionally: Those born under this angels influence can succeed as musicians, painters, writers, booksellers, editors and in graphics. Through art, music or painting, they will free people from negative energy and even from bad karma. They are defenders of culture, could be good novelists, historians and advisors. If they are painters, the paintings will tend to be sensitive or abstract.

Contrary Angel: Dominates gluttony, the neglect of the body, dirt, pessimism, prostitution, destructive criticism, the persecution complex and melancholy. A person under the influence of this angel may isolate themselves from society and become involved with cosmetic treatments or surgeries that damage the body.

Hierarchy: Powers
Archangel: Camael
Planet: Mercury
Power number: 4
Month of Change: April
Is present on Earth: from 13:00pm to 13:20pm
Incense: Sandlawood
Colour of Candle: Blue
Weekday: Tuesday
Crystal: Clear Quartz
Psalm: 87, verse

"The Lord shall count, when he write up the people, that this man was born there."

IERATHEL
Protects days: 01/02 - 15/04 - 27/06 - 08/09 - 20/11

Invoke this angel to help confuse the conspirators, protects against people who attack in court, and intervene in the propagation of light and the liberation of society.

Influence: Those born under Ierathel's influence are intelligent, balanced and mature. They are able to balance their individual instincts, accepting without necessarily following the advice and demonstrations of affection from everyone. They have strong initiative and perseverance, their life is clear and full of joy, maintaining a noble and refined appearance. They will have protection against any kind of negative force and their power of action is invincible. They will do everything so lucid and thoughtful, that their efforts usually lead to success. They will have an enormous capacity to know the future, either through spiritual guidance, dreams, astral projections, constantly reassessing their attitudes. They will advocate for the arts and sciences and they will mobilize large numbers of people for an ideal. They will be harmonious with a full view and understanding of the world.

Professionally: Those born under Ierathel's influence can be successful writers, journalists, social workers or any activity related to culture and leisure.

Contrary Angel: Dominates ignorance, intolerance and violence. A person under the influence of this contrary angel might otherwise be a proponent of authoritarian systems, supporting the exploitation of slave labour. They can practice barbarous acts and live in an inaccessible utopian world.

Hierarchy: Dominations
Archangel: Tsaphkiel
Planet: Venus
Power number: 11
Month of Change: November
Is present on Earth: from 08:00am to 09:00am
Incense: Rosemary
Colour of Candle: Blue
Weekday: Saturday
Crystal: Opal
Psalm: 139, verse 8

"If I ascend up into heaven, thou art there, if I make my bed in hell, behold thou art there."

IMAMAIAH
Protects days: 26/02 - 10/05 - 22/07 - 03/10 - 15/12

Invoke this angel to destroy the strength of enemies, people who only think of humiliating the weak and helps all who call for him to help obtain freedom. Protects travel in general and all who are desolate and lonely. This angel influences all things that are based on kindness and monetary gains from honest work.

Influence: Those born under Imamaiah's influence will have a vigorous and strong temperament, supporting any adversity with grace, patience and courage. Not afraid of work, but great inspiration to run it. They know how to handle any object and make works of great beauty. A woman under this angel's influence can be a great decorator, managing to capture the intuition with the angel's strengths in the home, through using the knowledge of magic symbols, different energies that will safeguard the home from negative influences. Those under the angel's influence respect people with morals, intelligence and feelings, knowing that these values ennoble the soul, and build a good life on Earth. They are always integrating the political and social affairs or inspire much confidence in other people. They have financial and material ability to project themselves, including internationally. They learn from mistakes, always teaching people the right way to act – experts in "fixing what is hopeless". They never get carried away by instinct, always thinking before acting. Optimistic, expansive and wise, they can rely on their lucky stars and the protection of their guardian angel.

Professionally: Those born under Imamaiah's influence may obtain success working as architects, constructions, engineering or management. They may be craftsmen of great reputation, known for the quality of work.

Contrary Angel: Dominates pride, blasphemy, cruelty, rudeness and fighting. A person under the influence of this contrary angel can be an impostor, bully, create fights, extremely nervous and use coarse and vulgar language.

Hierarchy: Principalities
Archangel: Haniel
Planet: Saturn
Power number: 12
Month of Change: December
Is present on Earth: from 17:00pm to 17:20pm
Incense: Jasmine
Colour of Candle: Pink
Weekday: Tuesday
Crystal: Pink Turmoline
Psalm: 87, verse 7

"As well the singers as the players on instrument shall be there: all my springs are in thee."

JELIEL

Protects days: 07/01 - 21/03 - 02/06 - 14/08 - 26/10

This angel is invoked to quell popular uprisings, to succeed against those who attack us in court and to restore marital bliss, bringing peace between spouses. This angel has power over employers and employees, helping to maintain harmony.

Influence: Those born under this angel's influence like to do everything quickly and when a child under Jeliel's influence does not have the patience to listen to teachers, it is because the information is already in their head. They have since childhood intuition for what is right or wrong. At heart, they believe that they are not on earth by chance and know that their family is karmicly connected so has certain feelings of being obligated to help them. Extremely loving, celebrates the universal truth and brotherly love. Their emotions are so strong, that they are experienced jointly by the angel. Never leaves a negative influence and has sobriety to dominate any situation. They will be the bringer of peace where there is conflict, defending the truth and hating violence. They love animals, flowers, forests and everything in nature. Probably has a name or surname of some Catholic saint and has "sanctified" protection. People consider them "magical" because of their good humour with which they solve the most varied of situations, always leaving a very good result. They are vain, like to embellish, to use expensive perfumes and dress fashionably.

Professionally: They can shine as a director, poet or working with aesthetics. This guardian angel shall, in their day to day, assist with their ability to speak and write.

Contrary Angel: Dominates selfishness, tyranny, callousness and meanness. Dominates those who mistreat animals, disunites spouses, it is perverse to parents, siblings, children, and causes intense love for oneself. If traveling outside the country, defies international law.

Hierarchy: Seraphim
Archangel: Metatron
Planet: Jupiter
Power number: 9
Month of Change: September
Is present on Earth: from 00:20am to 00:40am
Incense: Benzion
Colour of Candle: White
Weekday: Monday
Crystal: Aquamarine
Psalm: 21, verse 13

"Be thou exalted, LORD, in thine own strength: so will we sing and praise thy power."

LAOVIAH

Protects days: 16/01 - 30/03 - 11/06 - 23/08 - 04/11

Invoke this angel against fraud and to obtain victory. Influences the great historical figures and helps men obtain grace and recognition through their natural talent. The help of this angel will be provided through the experiences of life.

Influence: Those born under Laoviah's influence, will find many things that can be used practically in day-to-day life. They will be famous for their actions, improving their personality with each new experience in life. They will have strong feelings for their loved ones due to their intense ability to love. They will be successful and have financial stability. They will be fond of philosophy, will readily understand the world of elementals, and face major challenges, both in their sentimental and in professional life.

Professionally: People born under the influence of this angel will have success in any activity, because of their courage; no obstacle will be large enough to stop them. They will tend to be a star in political and social life. May act as a journalist or become a famous novelist. As a hobby can devote themselves to art, fashion, decoration and crafts.

Contrary Angel: Dominates rudeness, greed, jealousy and precipitation. A person under this contrary angels influence may not know how to win respect from others, may use slurs to eliminate competitors. They may act superficially and seek friendships only for financial interests. Have an exaggerated self-love, with a strong tendency towards narcissism.

Hierarchy: Cherubim
Archangel: Haziel
Planet: Saturn
Power number: 7
Month of Change: July
Is present on Earth: from 03:20am to 03:40am
Incense: Fennel
Colour of Candle: White
Weekday: Monday
Crystal: Amber
Psalm: 17, verse 15

"As for me, I will behold thy face in righteousness, I shall be satisfied, when I awake, with thy likeness."

LAUVIAH

Protects days: 22/01 - 05/04 - 17/06 - 29/08 - 10/11

Invoke this angel against the torments of the spirit, sadness and predisposition for good sleep. Favours the high sciences, discoveries and makes wonderful revelations in dreams.

Influence: Those born under Lauviah's influence, have the ability to understand symbolic messages and revelations. The astral world is manifested through the unconscious, experiencing visions, premonitions, or even images of higher worlds. Their psychic abilities are manifested in the small details, such as music, poetry, literature and philosophy. Their redemption on earth is very beautiful, because of their nobility of character; their spirit radiates a strong light. They know that the love in their heart can achieve anything, especially when the request is made for someone else in need. What they dream of they achieve. They can be the mainstay of their family or great support in the workplace. Their material things will be achieved through great struggle and at times even suffering. They have a nice reaction, friendly and comforting to people nearby. They will understand sadness, because they know the inner heart of the human being. They like spirituality, philosophy and will be educated people. Their guardian angel makes them do a lot of reading, of all types, from newspapers to the specialized books.

Professionally: People born under Lauviah's influence can have success in activities related to medicine, philosophy, esotericism and media or as a manufacturer of toys, electrical appliances, paper (books) or pharmaceutical products, mainly those related to sleep.

Contrary Angel: Dominates atheism, life and the pernicious lie. A person under the influence of this contrary angel may also be a false prophet or magician, a good "vivant", attacking spiritual dogma, to manufacture drugs evil, books or objects that defend erroneous doctrines.

Hierarchy: Thrones
Archangel: Tsaphkiel
Planet: Sun
Power number: 7
Month of Change: July
Is present on Earth: from 05:20am to 05:40am
Incense: Fennel
Colour of Candle: Light Green
Weekday: Monday
Crystal: Pyrite
Psalm: 8, verse 2

"Through the praise of the children and infants you have established a stronghold against your enemies, to silence the foe and the avenger."

LECABEL

Protects days: 05/02 - 19/04 - 01/07 - 12/09 - 24/11

Invoke this angel to protect people who work with agriculture and to get ideas in resolution of the toughest problems.

Influence: Those born under Lecabel's influence are endowed with great courage to face the most difficult obstacles, but need to be wary of power because abusing one's power is as harmful as brute force. They will have natural protection and fortune will come by their talent. They programme their higher self to connect with their inner self and it is a magnificent gift to study and apply their knowledge in nature, for the welfare of their community. They will appreciate the ancient books of history and archaeology. They will be very curious to know what would have happened in other incarnations, to be able answer the doubts of their soul and understand their existence. Their motto is "healthy mind in healthy body" and to achieve this balance, they can diet without eating red meat or chemical compounds and take up sports such as aerobics, weight training and cycling. They love nature and animals and will take care of animals with zeal – their house will be like a zoo. They tend to have a double life, living in the urban computerized world as well as farms at the same time, in direct contact with nature. Their main features are stability and rich interior, always loving the truth and order.

Professionally: Those born under Lecabel's influence maybe successful in the area of exact sciences, as a farmer, agronomist, and veterinarian or in activities related to astronomy and astrology.

Contrary Angel: Masters avarice, miserly, usury, lazy to study and illegal trade of animals. A person under the influence of this angel may be rowdy, mischievous, use force to dominate, have a great attraction to illicit love and practice illegal trade of toxic chemicals and drugs.

Hierarchy: Dominations
Archangel: Uriel
Planet: Sun
Power number: 11
Month of Change: November
Is present on Earth: from 10:00am to 10:20am
Incense: Camomile
Colour of Candle: Green
Weekday: Monday
Crystal: Garnet
Psalm: 70, verse 4

"Let all those that seek thee rejoice and be glad in thee and let such as love thy salvation say continually, let God be magnified."

LEHAHIAH
Protects days: 08/02 - 22/04 - 04/07 - 15/09 - 27/11

Invoke this angel to protect people crowned by divine love and to maintain harmony, peace and understanding.

Influence: Those born under Lehahiah's influence will be celebrated for their talents and actions. They will be inspired peacemakers, good people, they will have the sympathy of all because they love to solve their problems, always advising and supporting. Their aura of confidence attracts influential people who will invite them to work. They are good workers, earning more in positions of command. Their attitudes will be firm with high morals, kindness and hospitality, but can suffer disappointment when people do not match their expectations. They should always delve into all the subjects that interest them; otherwise they risk accommodating themselves or always have superficial knowledge about everything. Deeply emotional, transfers to their children the love received from parents. They may be a patron of the arts, especially music, because although they have musical talent are hardly practitioners. Have psychic gifts stored in the unconscious, which may be released in the practice of telepathy and clairvoyance. Perfect cleaning is one of their concerns, knowing that the negative miasma are impregnated in the dirt or broken objects. For life to pass by without any major obstacles it is necessary that everything is in order, nothing in decay.

Professionally: Those born under Lehahiah's influence maybe successful as a business administrator, poet, writer or working with oracles. Their hobby is certainly music.

Contrary Angel: Dominates discord, betrayal, stubbornness and folly. A person under the influence of this contrary angel may be biased by the facts, unscrupulous in business, excessive in exercise of dominion over the children and encourage sexual promiscuity and debauchery.

Hierarchy: Powers
Archangel: Camael
Planet: Saturn
Power number: 10
Month of Change: October
Is present on Earth: from 11:00am to 11:20am
Incense: Rosemary
Colour of Candle: Orange
Weekday: Sunday
Crystal: Onix
Psalm: 130, verse 5

"I wait for the Lord, my whole soul doth wait and in His word do I hope."

LELAHEL
Protects days: 05/02 - 19/04 - 01/07 - 12/09 - 24/11

Invoke this angel against people who are under negative influence and to obtain enlightenment in performing acts of healing. Lelahel masters the arts, fortune, science and love.

Influence: Those born under Lelahel's influence have the strength to cut negativity/evil (negative energies and entities). They are endowed with great idealism and balance. They are always ready to help people in need, and even make "sacrifices", acting disinterested. They bear a jewel called "inner light." Sometimes they can lack willpower, or even abandon the battlefield, but then there is the Renaissance, like a snake biting their own tail in order for regeneration. Always with their intelligence open and alert, making the word "impossible" not part of their dictionary. They feel the protection of God and the angelic world and may have strong psychic contact with their guardian angel; it is not difficult for them to contact intelligences from other galaxies (ET). They have the ability to capture messages and psychograph them, getting in tune with the other world (spiritualism) or even unconsciously moving objects. The unknown attracts and fascinates them. They develop scientific concepts that are sent from the Astral and may through analysis and study of traditional texts about angels, simplify them so that everyone can understand the beauty of science. They will work to get their name known and honoured by all and will use knowledge to great causes, especially to improve the standard of life, consciousness and culture of others. Adept in science and technology, will have unconventional ideas and suggestions to build prototype hospitals and techniques for spiritual healing or the use of crystals.

Professionally: Those born under Lelahel's influence maybe great astrologers or will opt for traditional or alternative medicine. They will obtain celebrity status in literature, specializing in fiction or futuristic themes. They may be famous artists, stars, always in the limelight. Being eternally loving, passionate, people will always put them on a pedestal. Their life will be amazing, always conquering their own space at home and at work.

Contrary Angel: Dominates prostitution, fraud, plagiarism, extortion and excessive ambition. Will be known in history as an ambitious person, dangerous, unbalanced and that gets nothing done. Exploit other people's money and could risk it all in fantastic and imaginary deals.

Hierarchy: Seraphim
Archangel: Metatron
Planet: Moon
Power number: 6
Month of Change: June
Is present on Earth: from 01:40am to 02:00am
Incense: Myrr
Colour of Candle: Yellow or Gold
Weekday: Sunday
Crystal: Tigers Eye
Psalm: 9, verse 2

"I will be glad and rejoice in thee, I will sing praise, O thou Most High."

LEUVIAH
Protects days: 24/01 - 07/04 - 19/06 - 31/08 - 12/11

Invoke this angel to help you attain the grace of God and act on memory and intelligence.

Influence: Those born under Leuviah's influence will be kind, cheerful, modest in their words and simple in their way of being. They will bear all adversity with patience and resignation, knowing that this is a form of material and spiritual evolution. They are extremely curious, always ready to learn and pass each experiment performed. They are culturally refined, love music, poetry and arts in general. They will have angelic protection against enemies, against those who try to harm them or using their name inappropriately. This protection is like a big wall of ethereal light, invisible to the eyes of ordinary people. They have complete control over the events of their life and attain the grace of God while remaining strong and determined to fight for their ideals.

Professionally: Those born under Leuviah's influence can achieve success in activities related to archaeology, museums and the preservation of memory of the past through archives and books. As a hobby can work with the manufacturing of objects to contact the angels or guides to develop and strengthen memory.

Contrary Angel: Masters immorality, heartbreak, loss, desperation and debauchery. A person under the influence of this contrary angel can use personal objects to work charms, negative energy, spells and amulets. They will be against social morals and interpret the archaic and sacred texts for evil. They may have an apocalyptic vision of the world.

Hierarchy: Thrones
Archangel: Tsaphkiel
Planet: Venus
Power number: 12
Month of Change: December
Is present on Earth: from 06:05am to 06:20am
Incense: Fennel
Colour of Candle: Yellow
Weekday: Monday
Crystal: Sapphire
Psalm: 39, verse 1

"I said, I will take heed to my ways, that I sin not with my tongue. I will keep my mouth with a bridle in the presence of the wicked."

MAHASIAH
Protects days: 10/01 - 24/03 - 05/06 - 17/08 - 29/10

Invoke this angel to live in peace with everyone. Mahasiah has control over philosophy, theology, the high sciences, arts and professions.

Influence: Those born under the influence of this angel learn everything easily and quickly, including languages, as it brings back memories of other incarnations. They are always transforming - being born, dying and being reborn - in all areas of their life, both sentimentally and professionally. They are an example of virtue and endowed with wisdom, generosity, a sense of justice and great inner balance. People born under Mahasiah's protection always act in accordance with the law, be it social or human law. Their truth is in their rationality, discussed through the study of philosophy. They will only serve their truth, which is God. They will spare no effort when it comes to spiritual growth, theirs or their families. Someone under this angel's influence will always retain awareness when using spirituality. They have the ability to work with spiritual energies and communicate with angels in order to serve the angelic world. They will like meditation centres, conferences, congresses and spiritual seminars. The bright light of their aura can be seen clearly around their shoulders and head. They tend to live in gentle ways. Their home may be spacious, clear and comfortable, filled with flowers and symbolic objects and probably have a large library.

Professionally: Those born under this angel's influence can succeed in the arts, using their refined taste and natural gift for this area, most likely in painting, decorating or working with objects of art.

Contrary Angel: Masters of ignorance, debauchery and all the bad qualities of the body (eating and drinking too much) and spirit (psychological disturbances). Someone dominated by this contrary angel may exploit the good faith of friends or family via superstition, use of spiritual wickedness or black magic. They may be religious fanatics, advocates of moral convention or talk about laws and dogmas without having understood or studied the subject. They can cynically consider themselves the best, with their good - but false - conduct.

Hierarchy: Seraphim
Archangel: Metatron
Planet: Venus
Power number: 12
Month of Change: December
Is present on Earth: from 1:20am to 1:40am
Incense: Lavender and Rosemary
Colour of Candle: White
Weekday: Monday
Crystal: Rose quartz
Psalm: 33, verse 4

"For the word of the LORD is right; and all his works are done in truth."

MANAKEL
Protects days: 12/03 - 24/05 - 05/08 - 17/10 - 29/12

Invoke this angel to help calm anger of people and take away all evil influences. Manakel influences inspiration for music and poetry. This angel dominates the world of the elementals.

Influence: Those born under Manakel's influence bring together the most beautiful qualities of soul and personality. They will be known for their great character, for their kindness and goodness to all people. They will bear all problems without complaining, have a clear conscience and always know when and how to act. As Eternal Fighters, they will be a positive stimulus for each person and the community. Their motto is "winning"! The unknown does not frighten them and they believe "you're only afraid to die, because you don't know how to live." Always vigilant, they can develop a strong power of abstraction (unconscious) and observation (conscious) and apply these powers in all situations. Always optimistic and logical in outlining plans, they spare no effort to realise these plans very successfully. Anyone under this angel's protection is a kind and skilful host, always on good terms with everyone due to their simplicity and the gentle way they listen with tenderness and care. They cannot hide their feelings from anyone. They must always hear the voice of their conscience and they are special beings who have God's protection.

Professionally: A person born under Manakel's influence will always be "inspired" to do any work, believing in their potential and never wasting any opportunity that arises in their life. Throughout their existence opportunities for projects in foreign countries will present themselves. Anyone under this angel's protection is inspired by music and poetry. With the help of their angel they will do work related to the elementals (water, fire, earth, wind).

Contrary Angel: Influences poor mental and moral qualities, satanic inspirations, concealment, anxiety, accommodation, discouragement, scandal and ingratitude. A person dominated by this contrary angel may be the bearer of only bad news, may pollute water or sacrifice animals.

Hierarchy: Angels
Archangel: Gabriel
Planet: Neptune
Power number: 7
Month of Change: July
Is present on Earth: from 21:40 to 22:00
Incense: Benzoin and Lavender
Colour of Candle: White
Weekday: Wednesday
Crystal: Amethyst
Psalm: 37, verse 22

"For such as be blessed of him shall inherit the earth; and they that be cursed of him shall be cut off."

MEBAHEL
Protects days: 19/01 - 02/04 - 14/06 - 26/08 - 07/11

This angel dominates justice, truth and freedom. Invoke Mebahel to help free people who feel trapped or depressed, to protect the innocent and those who do not know the truth.

Influence: Those born under this angel's influence will be knowledgeable coders of dreams (they decipher dreams with ease) of spiritual and material laws. Always the bearer of good news, they will be superb and selfless defenders of innocent people. Their ego and strong presence of mind will mark their day-to-day life, which they lead with nobility and dignity in their actions. Sometimes they will have a strong feeling of events occurring in other dimensions or other lives. Anyone under Mebahel's protection will have great adaptability and their life will be a transformation towards spiritual regeneration. They do not waste time with futile endeavours and will be the centre of attention in any environment for their wisdom, serenity and intuition. To enable them to assist others who need help, Mebahel seeks to show those under his influence knowledge, a legacy of other incarnations. In order to share their knowledge they will have the gift of oration and a strong ability of choice and discernment.

Professionally: A person born under this angel's influence can shine in advocacy, as the author of legal texts or specialising in cases which use historical myths to prove their thesis. Their struggle for a just society will be known and recognised internationally. They can promote acts against genocide and become "immortalised."

Contrary Angel: Masters the ability to lie and slander. Someone dominated by this contrary angel can use money to incriminate the innocent and help the guilty. They can speak of a connection that does not exist in the astral world. They may be an encoder of negative programmes or author of tough laws that would require sacrifices. They will have the ability to manipulate the gullible through scenic and technical effects, using negative energy. Experts in divorce, they could undermine arguments with false accusers.

Hierarchy: Cherubim
Archangel: Raziel
Planet: Jupiter
Power number: 6
Month of Change: June
Is present on Earth: from 4:20am to 4:40am
Incense: Myrrh
Colour of Candle: Lilac
Weekday: Thursday
Crystal: Amethyst
Psalm: 9, verse 10

"For such as be blessed of him shall inherit the earth; and they that be cursed of him shall be cut off."

MEBAHIAH
Protects days: 01/03 - 13/05 - 25/07 - 06/10 - 18/12

Invoke this angel to give encouragement and power to overcome any type of negative activity and for the protection of children.

Influence: Those born under Mebahiah's influence will be distinguished by their improvements, piety and zealous love of God and all mankind. They will know the path to follow, always in search of new perspectives. They will understand the divine mysteries, the doctrines of Christ and will spare no effort to plant them in the feelings of men. They are active proponents of religious, spiritual concepts and the preservation of morals. Where possible, they like to feel useful working for the welfare of the community. Their life will only fully unfold when they find the right partner that will be part of their journey through life. They feel the need to continue their existence through their children. They will understand life experiences and events, especially the unexpected, always solving them with new and creative ideas.

Anyone under the protection of this angel tends not to have any attachment to material things, which they consider to be no more than the result of dedication and persistence at work. They tend to be health conscious individuals who care about physical fitness. Their peaceful nature will be more impressive than their physique. Their angel is manifested spontaneously, when defending someone who has been wronged or when helping someone who has been hurt. People born under

Mebahiah's influence are enigmatic and have an aura of mystique around them which can lead to them being misunderstood.

Professionally: Those born under this angel's influence will have great facility for any activity in Human Resources or physical culture. They may be masters of alchemy.

Contrary Angel: Masters self-destruction and self-pity. A person dominated by this contrary angel will be the enemy of truth, propagator of false hopes that end in frustration for those who follow them. They may contribute to the destruction of missionaries who help humanity.

Hierarchy: Principalities
Archangel: Haniel
Planet: Jupiter
Power number: 8
Month of Change: August
Is present on Earth: from 18:00pm to 18:20pm
Incense: Violet
Colour of Candle: Pink
Weekday: Saturday
Crystal: Garnet
Psalm: 101, verse 6

"Mine eyes shall be upon the faithful of the land that they may dwell with me: he that walked in a perfect way, he shall serve me."

MEHIEL
Protects days: 10/03 - 22/05 - 03/08 - 15/10 - 27/12

Invoke this angel to protect against anger, hatred and accidents caused by unscrupulous people and traffic accidents. Mehiel encourages all who seek wisdom, teachers, authors and speakers, influencing those who love reading and all the bookstores that offer knowledge.

Influence: Anyone born under the influence of this angel will be a unique type and distinguished by the strength of their will to learn. They will be tolerant, generous, understanding of others, and people feel comfortable around them. They will always look for the good in people and understand their faults. A person born under Mehiel's protection will always seek to help everyone around them as they progress. Their wisdom will shine on others and they will be seen as a wise head on young shoulders. Enthusiastic and full of vitality, they will know how to balance reason and passion. Their main pleasure in life is to love and be loved (need to receive and give affection). Those born under this angel's influence always protect the family with the enormous power they have. At times they may seem naive, because they consider all as friends and do not understand betrayal. They get hurt easily, especially if treated unfairly. They will always be the centre of attention, because in addition to dressing splendidly, they are amazing at organising things such as travel, meetings or parties. They are always positive and even in times of difficulty believe that everything is in their favour. In their life there is no place for superstition or religion to believe in forces of destiny.

Professionally: Anyone born under Mehiel's protection can succeed by working as a journalist, editor, and writer or in public relations. They will have ability to work on the publishing and marketing of books.

Contrary Angel: Dominates those who try to convince others (controversy), literary disputes, criticism and megalomania. A person under the influence of this contrary angel may seek glory at any cost, even sacrificing other people and wasting their generosity with people who do not deserve it.

Hierarchy: Archangels
Archangel: Michael
Planet: Jupiter
Power number: 5
Month of Change: May
Is present on Earth: from 21:00pm to 21:20pm
Incense: Violet
Colour of Candle: Pink
Weekday: Saturday
Crystal: Garnet
Psalm: 101, verse 8

"I will early destroy all the wicked of the land; that I may cut off all wicked doers from the city of the LORD."

MELAHEL
Protects days: 28/01 - 11/04 - 23/06 - 04/09 -16/11

Invoke this angel to protect against weapons and assaults. Melahel dominates beauty and helps keep you safe when travelling. This angel influences nature, especially planting and knowledge of herbs to heal illnesses of the body.

Influence: Those born under Melahel's influence like to be absolutely correct, put everything in order and never defer what should be done. They have excellent communication skills and express their feelings clearly, although they may seem shy and introverted at first contact with strangers. They have strong premonitions about things that happen when least expected. They will be attracted to spiritualist philosophy and are enlightened souls. A person under this angel's protection is bold, capable of performing exotic tasks and undertaking different and dangerous expeditions. They are active ecologists and experts on healing plants. They have extraordinary intuition to know people's problems or their innermost secrets and can help with their knowledge of the secrets of plants. They believe that God is truly present in nature.

Professionally: Anyone born under Melahel's influence can succeed as a botanist, biologist, herbalist, biochemist, author of books on the virtues of plants and any activity related to plants and nature. They may live on ranches or farms, cultivating exotic and/or medicinal plants as a hobby.

Contrary Angel: Dominates lies, charlatanism and misuse of the knowledge of nature. A person under the influence of this contrary angel may be part of cults that encourage drug use, sell ineffective miracle potions, facilitate the spread of sexual diseases, grow noxious plants or spread the drug trade.

Hierarchy: Thrones
Archangel: Tsaphkiel
Planet: Moon
Power number: 7
Month of Change: July
Is present on Earth: from 7:20am to 7:40am
Incense: Eucalyptus
Colour of Candle: White
Weekday: Saturday
Crystal: Turquoise
Psalm: 120, verse 7

"I am for peace: but when I speak, they are for war."

MENADEL

Protects days: 10/02 - 24/04 - 06/07 - 17/09 - 29/11

Invoke this angel to maintain employment, maintain material assets acquired and help find lost property. Menadel protects against slander and helps people who feel depressed or have signs of depression. This angel helps give information about distant people we have not heard from.

Influence: Those born under the influence of Menadel will have a lot of willpower, be wise, confident and direct in speaking to others. They make excellent friends, partners and passionate lovers. They get offended easily with relatives and immediately criticise something they dislike. Anyone under this angel's protection acts wisely with discretion and assumes responsibility with seriousness and dedication. As perfectionists who are dedicated to their work, they expect the same attitude of the people they work with. In business they will be taken seriously and always reach their targets. At work their strong personality and charisma will make them known in the media, leading them to occupy a place of distinction. Optimistic, independent, active and advanced, they consider honesty and truth very important things in life. A person born under Menadel's influence does not believe in religion, but has faith in God. They may be called "prophet" by some for their profound vision of things, especially regarding social aspects. Despite knowing their ability to "abuse" the strength of their guardian angel, they will only ask assistance when all other avenues are exhausted, knowing that this force is too strong and sublime to be relied on for any need.

Professionally: Someone born under this angel's protection could be a great public speaker, scientist or researcher. A teacher or self-taught philosopher, they will teach the laws that regulate and govern the universe. They will defend their homeland with love and may be asked by political parties or the corporate community to participate in public life.

Contrary Angel: Dominates idleness and sloth. A person dominated by this contrary angel may adopt methods that hinder the progress of projects in justice, protect fugitive criminals or help them flee abroad to escape justice. They can be a false prophet and let themselves be worshipped.

Hierarchy: Powers
Archangel: Camael
Planet: Mars
Power number: 8
Month of Change: August
Is present on Earth: from 11:40am to 11:55am
Incense: Eucalyptus
Colour of Candle: Blue
Weekday: Wednesday
Crystal: Lapiz Lazuli
Psalm: 25, verse 8

"Good and upright is the LORD: therefore will he teach sinners in the way."

MIHAEL
Protects days: 22/02 - 06/05 - 18/07 - 29/09 - 11/12

Invoke this angel to help create peace and unity between spouses through talking. Mihael protects those who seek the Light, have premonitions or omens. This angel gives inspiration to unravel secrets and everything that needs to be discovered. Mihael facilitates friendship, marital fidelity and the generation of healthy Offspring.

Influence: Those born under this angel's influence will be peaceful, loving, have deep love for all and help preserve the welfare of the community. They will be a great organiser of social and political activities, promote reconciliation and broker negotiations. They are intellectuals and will defend the rights of women in society. As contributors of ideas related to community health care (e.g. nurses, Red Cross), they will be known even in other countries for their collaboration and dedication to the welfare of children. Someone under Mihael's protection will study marriage counselling through philosophy, religion, sociology or psychology. They consolidate relationships with friends or relatives with words of confidence and optimism. Their family will probably be noble and collaborative with their projects and desires. A person born under this angel's influence can have many children as they are passionate about a big family. Paternally demanding in matters of culture and studies, they know that where a broadening of consciousness and intelligence happens, more happiness and greater closeness to God ensues. They are accessible, honest, strong, and capable of tremendous resistance to fatigue and dedicated to hard work when prompted. Their mission on earth is humanitarianism. Anyone under Mihael's influence will live without prejudice of any kind, neither of class, race nor creed, and just have the sovereign truth as their friend. In their conduct in life they will always seek a neat pattern - this way they will show that life is easy to live and it is worth fighting for any ideal.

Professionally: Those born under this angel's influence have a good chance of working with trade associations, politics, public relations and advocacy. Their artistic talents may be inspired by nature and their enjoyment of outdoor life.

Contrary Angel: Induces divorce, produces the disunity of spouses, infidelity, multiple marriages and sterility. A person dominated by this contrary angel may be a prostitute, pimp, like sexual aberrations or stimulate pornography.

Hierarchy: Virtues
Archangel: Raphael
Planet: Venus
Power number: 5
Month of Change: May
Is present on Earth: from 15:40pm to 16:00pm
Incense: Jasmine
Colour of Candle: Very Pale Pink
Weekday: Saturday
Crystal: Rose Quartz
Psalm: 97, verse 2

"Clouds and darkness are round about him: righteousness and judgment are the habitation of his throne."

MIKAEL
Protects days: 16/02 - 30/04 - 12/07 - 23/09 - 05/12

Invoke this angel to assist you travelling safely. Mikael favours businessmen and people in high society. This angel helps unravel conspiracies and political or social disorders.

Influence: Those born under the influence of Mikael will be knowledgeable of techniques and means to run big companies and be distinguished by their diplomacy. They will have the protection of their guardian angel and are worthy, inspired and incorruptible. People in high places in social, economic or political circles will confide in them and collaborate closely with them with the aim to improve society. Anyone under this angel's protection will be popular, beloved of humble people and defend the innocent from wrong-doers. Their message is always one of optimism and faith, radiating cosmic energy with confidence, inspiration and creativity. They should take care in resolving situations without presumption and always use good sense. Throughout their lives, they will benefit tremendously from the light of this angel.

Professionally: A person born under Mikael's influence can be successful as a politician, diplomat, teacher, translator, entrepreneur or working with people from shows, festivals and ceremonies. Their pleasure for travel and knowledge of different languages may be useful in their work.

Contrary Angel: Masters perversity, treason, conspiracy, violence, scandal and drugs. Someone dominated by this contrary angel may spread false news and propaganda. Also create charitable companies that do not exist. They may be torturers or promoters of violent eroticism.

Hierarchy: Virtues
Archangel: Raphael
Planet: Mercury
Power number: 11
Month of Change: November
Is present on Earth: from 13:40pm to 14:00pm
Incense: Benjoin and Rosemary
Colour of Candle: White
Weekday: Monday
Crystal: Opal
Psalm: 120, verse 7

"I am for peace: but when I speak, they are for war."

MITZRAEL

Protects days: 06/03 - 05/18 - 30/07 - 11/10 - 23/12

Invoke this angel to help cure ills of the spirit and to facilitate freedom from persecution. Mitzrael influences fidelity and obedience.

Influence: Those born under this angel's influence will be distinguished by their talents and noble virtues. They have the finest qualities of body and soul. They know how to rectify their mistakes, because they believe it is through experiences that one builds character, the shell of the soul. People under Mitzrael's protection are always in search of their higher self, striving to achieve wisdom and an ideal balance. Their main quality is being a tireless worker. Living in a higher plain of existence, they know that by working for the social good they can get rid of their karma. Anyone born under this angel's influence can recognise the hand of God in every detail of nature. At a very early age they reach a high degree of maturity and are ready for success - not the success of stage or applause, but the most enduring one, fulfilling specific tasks on a day-to-day basis and being at peace with their conscience. They know how to live in the present and sow seeds for the future. They will be considered a symbol for mankind, both physically and spiritually.

Professionally: A person born under Mitzrael's influence may be known for their literary skills and great intelligence. Due to their great respect and admiration for nature, they can work in any area relating to nature, such as botany, gardening, biochemistry, pharmacy, flowers or ecology.

Contrary Angel: Masters insubordination, disobedience, infidelity, debauchery, alcohol, drugs and addictions in general. Someone dominated by this contrary angel may be religious yet still do harm to others. They may tend to break relationships impulsively, in a scandalous way.

Hierarchy: Angels
Archangel: Michael
Planet: Moon
Power number: 10
Month of Change: October
Is present on Earth: from 19:40pm to 20:00pm
Incense: Mint
Colour of Candle: White
Weekday: Tuesday
Crystal: Opal
Psalm: 144, verse 15

"Happy is that people, that is in such a case: yea, happy is that people, whose God is the LORD."

MUMIAH
Protects days: 18/03 - 30/05 - 11/08 - 23/10 - 04/01

Invoke this angel to protect against unknown mystical powers, to help have success and lead to discoveries that are generally useful. Mumiah dominates chemistry, physics, medicine, longevity and physical energy.

Influence: Those born under the influence of this angel will be celebrated for their wonderful discoveries. They will unveil the secrets of nature and have words of strength and courage against evil. They like new challenges that bring about change, as they are always renovating and revising their thinking. Everything is worn away, creating a new cycle and thus a new situation. Anyone under Mumiah's protection will dislike illusory things and strive to help people move away from oppression or depression. They search incessantly for the truth to reach a more objective state in life. They will have a superior force and trigger a series of events that could only happen because of their initiative or knowledge. Their spiritual power enables the divine light to intervene in the material world. People born under this angel always strive for an ideal and work magnificently, reserving special attention to the study of laws. They will attract wealth through the power of their words. Their spirituality and alchemical skills will manifest from childhood. They have deep knowledge of the relationship between microcosm and macrocosm.

Professionally: A person born under Mumiah's influence can be a judge with a reputation, a great lawyer, a student of nature, or they can work with elementals, alternative medicine or Eastern philosophies. They will be famous for their knowledge and dissemination of metaphysics.

Contrary Angel: Influences all beings that hate existence itself and would prefer to have never been born. Dominates despair; sterility, sadness, aggression, selfishness and rebellion with parents and relatives. Someone dominated by this contrary angel may have a pessimistic view of the world, criticise and mock those who cannot be stable in life or be an organiser of collective suicide.

Hierarchy: Angels
Archangel: Gabriel
Planet: Neptune
Power number: 11
Month of Change: November
Is present on Earth: from 23:40pm to 23:55pm
Incense: Chamomile
Colour of Candle: White
Weekday: Monday
Crystal: Smoked Quartz
Psalm: 114, verse 4

"The mountains skipped like rams, and the little hills like lambs."

NANAEL
Protects days: 27/02 - 11/05 - 23/07 - 04/10 - 16/12

Invoke this angel to protect the high sciences. Nanael influences clergymen, teachers, magistrates and men who work with the law.

Influence: Those born under this angel's protection will be distinguished by knowing the abstract sciences, love the quiet life, peace, meditation and listening to classical music. They are enlightened people and you will see innocence and truth in them. They may have a spiritual vocation or possess metaphysical knowledge. People under Nanael's influence are trustworthy and never act recklessly. They enjoy strong relationships and will be the one friend everyone would love to have. Endowed with great affection, they live in the light of love and all that is beautiful touches them. Being traditionalists, they give much importance to marriage and children. Generally more active than passionate, they know how to control their instincts without repressing them. Their intelligence is developed more by experience than by studies. Anyone born under this angel's protection likes success and tends to build beautiful things for altruistic purposes. Their family will be part of a large project and they do not measure effort to win a place in the sun. Their prestige does not feed their vanity. They will live within reality and dedicate themselves fully to live a peaceful existence, with much effort, dedication and doing everything perfectly and in a clean way. They may have encountered health problems in childhood or adolescence, yet in spite of their physical frailty they have the spirit of a very agile warrior. They are known to enjoy the finer things in life, without thereby having to commit thoughtless acts to get them. They are the pillar that sustains humanity.

Professionally: Those born under Nanael's influence can achieve success in activities related to foreign countries, such as import/export, diplomacy, cultural exchanges or technological cooperation.

Contrary Angel: Dominates ignorance, sorrow, sadness, laziness, guilt and punishment. A person under the influence of this contrary angel will not care for their appearance, be unable to work for free for any worthy cause and may be obsessed with material goods.

Hierarchy: Principalities
Archangel: Haniel
Planet: Saturn
Power number: 6
Month of Change: June
Is present on Earth: from 17:20pm to 17:40pm
Incense: Sandalwood
Colour of Candle: White
Weekday: Monday
Crystal: Sapphire
Psalm: 118, verse 5

"I called upon the LORD in distress: the LORD answered me, and set me in a large place."

NELCHAEL
Protects days: 26/01 - 09/04 - 21/06 - 02/09 - 14/11

Invoke this angel to destroy the enemy's power or slander against people who use negative energy to benefit themselves against the innocent. Nelchael influences astronomy, astrology, geology, mathematics and all sciences.

Influence: Those born under this angel's protection show great composure, use words in moderation and balance the spiritual with the material. Self-controlled and patient, they have strong leadership skills. They search for financial stability, pursue an ideal at any cost, not accepting losses. Endowed with great intelligence and imagination, they have maturity and mastery over themselves. A person under Nelchael's influence always seeks to harmonise all the family, although often feels misunderstood by their relatives. Having the tendency to be a loner, they are nevertheless always in search of their perfect match. They love the beautiful and hate what is ugly and vulgar. They are refined, lovers of poetry and painting, and like to present people with flowers. People under this angel's protection will be very loved and respected in their workplace. They can search for scientifically transcendental knowledge through readings of ancient texts, decoded with the use of information technology. Their mission is to unite science and art with religion. They like to develop their mediumship through the esoteric sciences, but always in an analytical way. They are of the view "seeing is believing".

Professionally: Those born under Nelchael's influence can achieve success teaching mathematics, geometry, computing, administration, geography or philosophy, or work as a psychologist or social worker.

Contrary Angel: Dominates error, ignorance, prejudice, aggression and violence. A person under the influence of this contrary angel may facilitate the enactment of erroneous laws. In their vision of the future, they may work only for the machine, negating the value of man within the company.

Hierarchy: Thrones
Archangel: Tsaphkiel
Planet: Mercury
Power number: 5
Month of Change: May
Is present on Earth: from 6:40am to 7:00 am
Incense: Lavender
Colour of Candle: Lilac
Weekday: Monday
Crystal: Amethyst
Psalm: 30, verse 5 and 6

"For his anger endured but a moment; in his favour is life: weeping may endure for a night, but joy cometh in the morning. And in my prosperity I said, I shall never be moved."

NEMAMIAH
Protects days: 03/03 - 15/05 - 27/07 - 08/10 - 20/12

Invoke this angel to help everyone who works for a just cause, to thrive in all areas and to liberate people with addictions, leading them towards a healthy life. Nemamiah favours those who work in coastal cities and all who carry out functions related to the recreation area at these locations.

Influence: Those born under this angel's influence will love to be placed in a leadership position and endure fatigue with patience and courage. Distinguished by their bravery, they have plenty of guts and willpower. Having a great love for all things, they work to improve society and tend to abolish the privileges and resources of undeserving people. Having protection from betrayal or revenge, they have good luck in foreign travel. People under Nemamiah's protection will be fighters against the forces of evil through their culture and intelligence. They always strive to come up with ideas for a new world, battling against lower levels of consciousness. Knowledge of their guardian angel's presence is central to their lives, making their existence on earth better. A person under this angel's influence will have great revelations in dreams, defend all good causes and will be called to lay the foundation for new theories. They will be seen as great economists or administrators, especially in times of crisis. Cheerful, active and friendly, they are always the centre of attention in all situations. Fond of everything and everybody, they love family life and devote special attention to their children.

Professionally: Anyone born under Nemamiah's influence is called to leadership of political parties, labour unions or businesses and will participate in parades or fanfares which will attract students and observers, delighting the population with their attention to detail; they will be a good cartoonist, writer of anecdotes or of children's stories. They can specialise in finding placements for people who need work.

Contrary Angel: Dominates cowardice, treason, fraud and slander. A person under the influence of this contrary angel may distort the view of all things, always be in disagreement with any opinion or create friction among leaders. They may use their intelligence for evil and be a specialist in placing fault with others.

Hierarchy: Archangel
Archangel: Michael
Planet: Mars
Power number: 10
Month of Change: October
Is present on Earth: from 18:40pm to 19:00pm
Incense: Eucalyptus
Colour of Candle: Green
Weekday: Saturday
Crystal: Amazonite
Psalm: 113, verse 9

"He makes the barren woman to keep house, and to be a joyful mother of children. Praise ye the LORD."

NITH-HAIAH

Protects days: 30/01 - 13/04 - 25/06 - 06/09 - 18/11

Invoke this angel to help you find the truth in esoteric mysteries. Nith-haiah dominates revelations and influences peace by knowing the truth. A person under the influence of this angel likes to practice "esoteric teachings", following the divine laws.

Influence: Those born under this angel's influence have serenity, balance, harmony, self-control, moderation and patience. This is why it is easier for them than for others to achieve emotional stability as well as professional and material progress. Benevolent even with their enemies, they have joy and pleasure in living and live life to the fullest. Their life has no locks or limits. Usually self-taught, they are well informed on any subject. People under Nith-haiah's protection can have great psychic power and inspiration to dominate the esoteric sciences. They can have curiosity about the science of evil in order to be able to counteract negativity through kindness and the good. They know and understand the prayers to summon elementals (water, fire, earth, air), make revelations through charisma and influence people's behaviour. They love peace, solitude, contemplation and the mysteries of nature. As a child they will understand the meaning of things gained not through questioning but through observation. They will have the protection of the ancestors.

Professionally: A person born under this angel's influence can be successful as a psychologist, writer, scientist, or in any activity related to esotericism.

Contrary Angel: Dominates black magic (Satan worship), wickedness and prostitution. Someone ruled by this contrary angel may use the forces of evil for vengeance, make pacts with demons, be the author of formulas for enchantment, use animals in ritual sacrifice, harm nature (humans, animals and products of the land) or indulge in sexual depravity

Hierarchy: Domination
Archangel: Tsadkiel
Planet: Saturn
Power number: 11
Month of Change: November
Is present on Earth: from 8:00am to 8:20am
Incense: Rosemary and Sandalwood
Colour of Candle: Lilac
Weekday: Sunday
Crystal: Amethyst
Psalm: 9, verse 2

"I will be glad and rejoice in thee: I will sing praise to thy name, O thou most High."

NITHAEL

Protects days: 28/02 - 29/02 - 12/05 - 24/07 - 05/10 -
17/12

Invoke this angel to help you attain the mercy of God and longevity. Nithael protects heads of states, presidents, monarchs, princes, and all people who devote their lives to spirituality and charity. This angel favours the continuation and legacy of families and business stability. Nithael assists people who need help from individuals in high places and provides a quiet and safe existence.

Influence: Those born under the influence of this angel will be celebrated for their writings and their eloquence. They have a great reputation and will be distinguished by their merits and virtues, gaining the confidence to fill key posts both in government and private companies. They will be destined to assume leadership positions, due to their broad vision for understanding things and for avoiding evil. A person under Nithael's protection will be the very embodiment of goodness, order, justice and legality. With a strong personality, great authority and prestige, they will bring awareness of angels on earth. They have knowledge of spirituality and metaphysics. They are endowed with a faculty that only special people have, being able to turn anything they want into reality. They enthusiastically defend the good against evil and will be discreet when making judgments or offering spiritual guidance. They will be different to others as children, especially because of their beauty and grace in the way they carry themselves. Their aura is bright and they conduct themselves with goodness.

Professionally: Those born under the influence of this angel have a tendency to become senior spiritual dignitaries, lawyers or great doctors. If they follow a political career, they may provide service in a constituent assembly. They are likely to be major artists whose works will become a hallmark of their time. Their life will be marked by hard work. As an employer or successful entrepreneur, they will create jobs for many people, including relatives.

Contrary Angel: Dominates conspiracy, betrayal and the accumulation of anger. A person under the influence of this contrary angel might have a sharp tongue, make written defamatory statements, and cause ruin of business, humiliation or sacrifice of those less fortunate.

Hierarchy: Principalities
Archangel: Haniel
Planet: Jupiter
Power number: 5
Month of Change: May
Is present on Earth: from 17:40pm to 18:00pm
Incense: Chamomile
Colour of Candle: Light Yellow
Weekday: Friday
Crystal: Tigers Eye
Psalm: 102, verse 19

"For he hath looked down from the height of his sanctuary; from heaven did the LORD behold the earth;"

OMAEL
Protects days: 04/02 - 18/04 - 30/06 - 11/09 - 23/11

Invoke this angel to help people who are desperate to have more patience. Omael dominates the protection of the animal kingdom and influences the perpetuation of species and breeds. This angel influences chemists, physicians and surgeons.

Influence: Those born under Omael's influence are extremely fair and live in harmony with the universe. Being protected by this angel they will have steady confidence in themselves and will always fight for great ideals. They love animals, nature and humans with great sincerity. They have good general knowledge and are always reviewing a situation in search of a more objective view. Angels predict victory, success and achievement in every way, but it is up to each person to choose to walk on the lines of destiny.

Professionally: Anyone born under this angel's protection can be successful as a paediatrician, obstetrician, surgeon, or in any political activity relating to childcare, anatomy or chemistry.

Contrary Angel: Dominates indifference, violence against animals, the spread of bugs and monstrous phenomena. A person under the influence of this contrary angel may be in favour of fascist ideas, manufacture deadly chemicals to cause destruction, be in favour of euthanasia, deny their children or feel irresistible sexual attraction to children and adolescents.

Hierarchy: Dominations
Archangel: Uriel
Planet: Sun
Power number: 6
Month of Change: June
Is present on Earth: from 9:40am to 10:00am
Incense: Roses
Colour of Candle: Green
Weekday: Thursday
Crystal: Emerald
Psalm: 70, verse 4

"Let all those that seek thee rejoice and be glad in thee: and let such as love thy salvation say continually, Let God be magnified."

PAHALIAH
Protects days: 25/01 - 08/04 - 20/06 - 01/09 - 13/11

Invoke this angel to help you discover all the mysteries of spirituality and help achieve a closer connection with the divine. Pahaliah dominates spirituality, theology and morality and helps you find the right vocation.

Influence: Those born under this angel's influence develop a very strong personality early on and are true fighters, always striving for high ideals. They are great optimists, masters of the art of discernment and like to live in peace with everyone. This brings all the experiences they have ever had to life, especially those relating to family and children. They do not know how to live alone and need a faithful companion in order to be happy. People under Pahaliah's protection look younger than they actually are and have a character that portrays abundance regardless of their financial situation. Their angel influences them in a very energetic way when they become lazy in any situation. Working together with the angels will help them materially. They will explore spirituality and understand the invisible world as harmoniously as the visible. They will be intellectuals, scholars of various topics.

Professionally: A person born under this angel's influence may follow a career in journalism or any other area of social communication. They could be great preachers, who live on oratory, speeches and lectures.

They have skill in crafts or activities relating to antiquities. They can also work with esotericism.

Contrary Angel: Anyone who lets himself be dominated by this contrary angel may be a religious fanatic or bigot, libertine or explorer of prostitution. They could financially harm people of good faith and may be unable to capture the spirituality that exists in people. They may be selfish, the withholder of truth, dictating to those who do not usually follow.

Hierarchy: Thrones
Archangel: Tsaphkiel
Planet: Moon
Power number: 13
Month of Change: January and April
Is present on Earth: from 6:20am to 6:40 am
Incense: Jasmine
Colour of Candle: White
Weekday: Thursday
Crystal: Moonstone
Psalm: 119, verse 2

"Blessed are they that keep his testimonies and that seek him with the whole heart"

POIEL

Protects days: 02/03 - 14/05 - 26/07 - 07/10 - 19/12

Invoke this angel to help favour the acquisition of prestige and wealth or to spread major philosophies.

Influence: Those born under the influence of Poiel will be appreciated by everyone because of their modesty and pleasant mood. Their fortune will be obtained due to their talent and good conduct. They can get everything they want and will always be committed to learn and know all things in the world. Despite their modest and fragile appearance, will fight to put themselves in a favourable socio-economic position and thereby gain recognition for their extraordinary talent, becoming known worldwide. Their openness to all will be a symbol of vitality and generosity. Someone under the protection of this angel will know how to balance reason and passion. They believe in the salvation of people through love and are always ready to help everyone. They always work according to angelic and spiritual philosophy. As optimists they know how to emphasise the positive qualities of people and situations. With their charm they illuminate the lives of everyone around them.

Professionally: It is easy for a person born under Poiel's influence to shine in foreign lands, understand different languages, cultures and customs. They also have great willingness to work with spirituality, always for good.

Contrary Angel: Dominates ambition, pride, aggression and incoherence. A person under the influence of this contrary angel might dress in a ridiculous manner, organise international smuggling, rise at the expense of others' work, falsify signatures on documents or cheques or lead others to consider them the greatest of all masters.

Hierarchy: Principalities
Archangel: Aniel
Planet: Sun
Power number: 10
Month of Change: October
Is present on Earth: from 18:20pm to 18:40pm
Incense: Myrrh and Patchouli
Colour of Candle: White
Weekday: Tuesday
Crystal: Pyrite
Psalm: 144, verse 4

"Man is like to vanity: his days are as a shadow that passed away."

REHAEL
Protects days: 13/02 - 27/04 - 09/07 - 20/09 - 02/12

Invoke this angel to protect against negativity or to make people recognise their actions and attain divine mercy. Rehael helps attain peace, good health and long life. This angel influences parental love, filial respect and obedience of children towards their elders.

Influence: Those born under Rehael's influence will be aware of the need for regeneration of matter, so there can be an increase in spirituality. They will feel altruistic love for all men on Earth, whom they regard as God's children. They have the gift of healing, which they use exceptionally, healing either with their hands or mentally, through prayers or emanations of positive thoughts. Their truth is eternal, fulfilling their karmic mission of defeating evil along with their contrary angels. Someone under Rehael's protection is always exploring ways or methods of stopping evil. They believe in miracles, understanding that they happen through divine mercy. Their optimism is contagious and they will always be fine with everyone. They are highly enlightened, strong participants and believe that man can overcome all obstacles by using their intelligence. They will love their children and certainly do everything to train and direct them in life.

Professionally: A person born under this angel's influence can succeed as a doctor, nurse, sociologist, professor or writers. They may provide laboratory services, work in geriatric clinics or research for the discovery of drugs to prolong life and isolate diseases.

Contrary Angel: Masters severity, cruelty, violence, alcoholism and prostitution of children. A person dominated by this contrary angel might be driven to despair and suicide, or commit infanticide or genocide.

Hierarchy: Powers
Archangel: Camael
Planet: Saturn
Power number: 9
Month of Change: September
Is present on Earth: from 12:40pm to 13:00 pm
Incense: Lavender
Colour of Candle: Pink
Weekday: Thrusday
Crystal: Rose Quartz
Psalm: 29, verse 11

"The LORD will give strength unto his people; the LORD will bless his people with peace."

REYEL
Protects days: 03/02 - 17/04 - 29/06 -10/09 - 22/11

Invoke this angel against heretics and people who harm us, consciously or unconsciously. Reyel dominates all spiritual emotions and meditations.

Influence: Those born under this angel's influence are divined and will be distinguished by their qualities, for their zeal in propagating the truth and destroying false and slanderous writings. Their conduct is exemplary, embracing love, truth, peace, justice, tradition, freedom and silence. A person under Reyel's protection will follow rules according to their conscience and may run charities or spiritual organisations with the motto of no corruption. They always take the right path and their existence on earth is always at a very high level of integrity, which can be noticed without knowing why. The rewards for their efforts are great renewal of life and release of negative karmic ties. Their life is a celebration, illuminated by their spiritual choice. They need to be careful not to create feelings of guilt in relation to family problems, because all are undergoing an evolution without loss but with renewal. Their house is always clean, tidy, decorated with flowers and radiating the fragrance of incense.

Professionally: Anyone born under this angel's influence can be successful as a painter, sculptor or writer as Reyel manifests through art and painting.

Contrary Angel: Dominates fanaticism, hypocrisy, selfishness and racial prejudice. A person under the influence of this contrary angel may be suspicious of the good faith of others and ridicule everyone using the term "circus" or "clown" for people who like and want to help transform philosophies or religion.

Hierarchy: Domination
Archangel: Uriel
Planet: Mars
Power number: 8
Month of Change: August
Is present on Earth: from 12:40 to 13:00 pm
Incense: Sandalwood and Roses
Colour of Candle: Blue
Weekday: Wednesday
Crystal: Lapis Lazuli
Psalm: 53, verse 6

"Oh that the salvation of Israel were come out of Zion! When God brings back the captivity of his people, Jacob shall rejoice, and Israel shall be glad."

ROCHEL

Protects days: 01/01 - 15/03 - 27/05 - 08/08 - 20/10

Invoke this angel to help you find objects or people, including missing ones, and to show you who stole or hid them, if applicable. Angel Rochel assists to achieve fame, fortune and success in economics, politics or justice.

Influence: Those born under this angel's influence will be endowed with strength and energy, always acting in a manner beneficial to others. They have a wonderful inventive genius and a strong mission to meet with the family. With their amazing ability to participate in the suffering of loved ones they gain great spiritual treasures. People under Rochel's protection are endowed with strong intuition, which manifests itself through analytical intelligence. With their great adaptability and willingness to learn, they are never afraid to face new evidence nor give up on their goals. If necessary, angels will indicate a new path to them. Never giving into temptation for material things, they understand that every loss on the physical plane is a victory on the spiritual plane.

Professionally: Anyone born under this angel's influence can be a great economist, lawyer, judge, politician or work with foreign trade. As a great orator, their talents will be at the service of good causes.

Contrary Angel: Masters unnecessary costs, interminable processes, false laws, stubbornness and selfish impulses. A person dominated by this contrary angel might have tendency to be dramatic, cause destruction to families or manipulate laws for their own benefit.

Hierarchy: Angels
Archangel: Gabriel
Planet: Jupiter
Power number: 12
Month of Change: December
Is present on Earth: from 22:40pm to 23:00pm
Incense: Rosemary
Colour of Candle: Yellow
Weekday: Monday
Crystal: Sapphire
Psalm: 15, verse 5

"He that; putted not out his money to usury, nor take reward against the innocent. He that doeth these things shall never be moved."

SEALIAH
Protects days: 19/02 - 03/05 - 07/15 -26/09 - 08/12

Invoke this angel to help confuse the proud and wicked that oppress the humble. Sealiah raises good will and hope when someone is in despair, dominates vegetation and everything that lives and breathes. This angel influences the elementals that care for and protect nature.

Influence: Those born under the influence of angel Sealiah will be connected to details - their house will be decorated with miniatures, figurines or small pictures in good taste. Their garden will have abundant vegetation, sheltering small animals. They will always have money for their needs and the word crisis does not exist in their vocabulary. Endowed with prodigious culture, they share their knowledge and experiences with those who have similar ideas. By discovering their spiritual truth, they can produce amazing changes in their neighbourhood or community. People under Sealiah's protection will study the scriptures and discover the true laws of spirituality. They have a gift for making mysterious revelations, through oracles, dreams or premonitions. For the greatness of their heart they will increase the light in anyone around them and create a strong cosmic bond with the angels. Their role on earth will be to help society discover that angelic power lies in a plane of light and we are allowed to know of their existence. They are instructed to "rekindle" the spirituality in everyone.

Professionally: Someone born under the influence of this angel may succeed in activities that allow them to always be in contact with people, due to their willingness to help everyone. They often work in charities or recovery of people marginalised by society.

Contrary Angel: Masters imbalance, coldness and evil. A person dominated by this contrary angel may be an agitator in strikes, dependent on tranquilizers or deny help to the humble and needy.

Hierarchy: Virtues
Archangel: Raphael
Planet: Sun
Power number: 7
Month of Change: July
Is present on Earth: from 14:40pm to 15:00pm
Incense: Rosemary
Colour of Candle: White
Weekday: Monday
Crystal: Clear Quartz
Psalm: 93, verse 1

"The LORD reigned, he is clothed with majesty; the LORD is clothed with strength, wherewith he hath girded himself: the world also is established, that it cannot be moved."

SEHEIAH
Protects days: 02/02 - 16/04 - 28/06 - 09/09 - 21/11

Invoke this angel to assist against torments, diseases and parasites. Seheiah also protects against fires, evil and ruin of business. This angel promotes a long life.

Influence: Those born under Seheiah's influence will have common sense, act with prudence and wisdom, and be authentic and true. Resist all with dignity and everything in their life will work flawlessly. They always do well in the most chaotic situations as with the help of their angel bright ideas emerge suddenly. His spiritual strength is closely linked to the healing angels and even unknowingly, unconsciously, it helps improve human suffering. They always have a word of optimism to help people (especially family) in any insecure situation because they are always in tune with all divine forces. Has misgivings when it comes to travel. If their heart says it's better to hear it.

Professionally: Those born under Seheiah's influence maybe successful working in areas related to public administration, writing books, materials, radio and television or in studies of homeopathy and acupuncture.

Contrary Angel: Masters disasters, accidents, negligence, and disorganization. People under this influence can harm their peers, making careless use of beauty products (silicone injections, permanent makeup) or participating in the production of defective equipment, to cheapen production. Often not reflecting before acting, causing insecurity among all who live. May cause fires due to their negligent attitude.

Hierarchy: Dominations
Archangel: Uriel
Planet: Jupiter
Power number: 6
Month of Change: June
Is present on Earth: from 09:00am to 09:20am
Incense: Frankincense
Colour of Candle: Deep Green
Weekday: Thrusday
Crystal: Amazonite
Psalm: 70, verse 5

"But I am poor and needy, make haste unto me, Oh God: thou art my help and my deliverer; Oh Lord, make no tarrying."

SITAEL
Protects days: 08/01 - 22/03 - 03/06 - 15/08 - 27/10

Invoke this angel to succeed against all odds and to protect against car accidents, assaults and weapons. Sitael dominates being noble, personal magnetism and great discoveries.

Influence: Those born under the influence of this angel know they have much luck and thus have the possibility to succeed financially. They are always active, fighting for their ascension. Their pride prevents them from asking for favours from anyone. They are lone fighters. People under Sitael's protection are beautiful inside and out, their strong charisma attracting the attention of others. They breathe life and live every day in a special way. They are not very fond of the word "destiny", as they like to live one day at the time. They are great souls and like to have many friends, who usually give them valuable advice. Being very knowledgeable makes it easy for them to understand all of life's situations. Having great sympathy and kindness, they usually forgive people who try to harm them. Anyone born under Sitael's influence will be a great transformer, protecting and encouraging people with new ideas. They love parties, banquets and celebrations; although they are very reserved in the way they dress and can sometimes be a little shy due to all the experiences that the world offers. They speak their mind as they don't know how to conceal their feelings or act in a dubious way. They have many memories of things that were not experienced in this incarnation and which usually appear in the form of their nobility is the envelope of their soul.

Professionally: A person born under this angel's influence will do well in positions of administration, management, ministries, as heads of offices or sections. They may be great lecturers or political figures. Angel Sitael asks those born under his protection for more patience, to think carefully before speaking and to act with prudence and caution in all aspects of life.

Contrary Angel: Master of hypocrisy, perjury, lying, ingratitude and erotic rituals. A person dominated by this contrary angel may blame fate for everything bad that happens in their life and pass their responsibilities to others. They do not help anyone and then charge aggressively (attack) at those under their protection. They may have a poor appearance, have many amorous adventures or use sexuality to get into high positions.

Hierarchy: Seraphim
Archangel: Metatron
Planet: Sun
Power number: 11
Month of Change: November
Is present on Earth: from 00:40am to 01:00am
Incense: Patchouli
Colour of Candle: Orange
Weekday: Monday
Crystal: Agate
Psalm: 90, verse 2

"Before the mountains were brought forth, or ever thou had formed the earth and the world, even from everlasting to everlasting, thou art God."

UMABEL

Protects days: 07/03 - 19/05 - 31/07 - 12/10 - 24/12

Invoke this angel to help you be the friend of a person. Umabel encourages the study of astrology, psychology and esoteric science. The angel strongly influences people to specialise and excel in research in these areas.

Influence: Those born under Umabel's influence will love to travel and have fun, are very loving and sensitive. They are aware of how to act and their intelligence is at the service of angelic powers. Introverted and affectionate, they do not adapt to sudden changes. As traditionalists they are loyal and devoted to the values transmitted and taught by parents. Endowed with great intuition, they are open to things that are around, despite not getting involved. In order to feel comfortable in a social position or at work, they are driven by a need for spiritual faith, requiring ideological support. Someone under this angel's protection will not like aggressive or undecided people. They are patient to the extreme and capable of supporting everyone, from a lover to a family member. They are not interested in changing the situation of a group or social class by investing all their energies in people who have a closed heart/mind or in a particular case. When they do not receive affection, they prefer isolation. Their life force is manifested in paternity or maternity. They are stable and they search for the same image of civility in people. They will be loved for their balance, sweetness, kindness and warmth. They organise their life according to their conscience, freely expressed through good deeds and fellowship.

Professionally: Anyone born under angel Umabel's influence can be a great psychologist and adapts well with children. They can achieve success by channelling their emotions into novels or poetry. Their work with astrology and oracles will bring them accomplishments.

Contrary Angel: Masters debauchery, indifference and infidelity. A person dominated by this contrary angel might acquire inharmonious vices contrary to nature, isolate themselves to the extreme, lie to themselves for not being able to face reality, self-destruct or have an unhealthy dependency on their mother or father.

Hierarchy: Archangels
Archangel: Michael
Planet: Venus
Power number: 7
Month of Change: July
Is present on Earth: from 20:00pm to 20:20pm
Incense: Sage and Eucalyptus
Colour of Candle: Light Green
Weekday: Saturday
Crystal: Rose Quartz
Psalm: 112, verse 2

"His seed shall be mighty upon earth: the generation of the upright shall be blessed."

VASAHIAH

Protects days: 06/02 - 20/04 - 02/07 - 13/09 - 25/11

Invoke this angel to protect against those who attack us in court. Vasahiah is an angel of justice and influences jurists, lawyers and judges. This angel also promotes grace and mercy for big businessmen.

Influence: Those born under Vasahiah's influence will be lovely, modest and spiritual. They have excellent memory and speak any language with ease. They will be great scholars and their life will be rich in experience and variety. People born under this angel's protection want everyone to have the same opportunities in life regardless of race, creed or culture. Their word is an order to be respected. They have the gift of words and it is easy for them to speak in public. They are invincible when speaking with superiors to defend the less fortunate. Overcoming obstacles is just part of their mission. As they live a full life they will always remain balanced internally. Their appearance may at times seem austere, as they are an example of great responsibility toward their fellow man, against those who act in bad faith. They will be active warriors of their guardian angel, by taking swift actions and never deferring their decisions.

Professionally: Those born under this angel's influence can be successful as lawyers, social workers, teachers, writers or in producing books, abstracts, hand-outs or any other objects or tools created to help the layman, which would otherwise be impossible by normal means.

Contrary Angel: Dominates irresponsibility, malice and hatred. A person under the influence of this contrary angel may be a genius of evil, corrupt spiritual teachings, misuse sacred texts or misinterpret the law.

Hierarchy: Domination
Archangel: Uriel
Planet: Mercury
Power number: 8
Month of Change: August
Is present on Earth: from 10:20 to 10:40 am
Incense: Chamomile
Colour of Candle: Emerald Green
Weekday: Monday
Crystal: Emerald
Psalm: 32, verse 4

"For day and night thy hand was heavy upon me: my moisture is turned into the drought of summer. Selah"

VEHUEL
Protects days: 23/02 - 07/05 - 19/07 - 30/09 - 12/12

Invoke this angel to help people connect with God, for the glorification of all people and the admiration of the heavenly kingdom.

Influence: Those born under Vehuel's influence will be distinguished by their talents and virtues. Their great generosity can be seen in their aura. They will be cherished by all good people who possess the same qualities and virtues. As faithful executors of noble causes they encourage people to follow good conduct by their example. They fight for the glory of God. They are beloved of the Divine Will for their ease in forgiving the mistakes of others, whoever they are. People born under this angel's protection are very prudent in their judgement. With a sense of humour they can criticise without arrogance to awaken people. They are dynamic, innovative, intelligent and fair, although individualistic. They will find it easy to express themselves to people of any social class because of their great depth of mind. After marriage they become more stable and their family will be united and harmonious. Physically slender and elegant, refined and intellectually open, people might consider it "difficult" to deceive them. Someone under Vehuel's influence has social recognition, which proves that life is only "hard" for those who cannot take the opportunities offered to them. They are endowed with great moral virtue; they do not like people who miss their appointments. Their maturity on earth is as noble as their character.

Professionally: Those born under the influence of this angel can be brilliant writers, are very creative and have respect for spirituality. Due to their enormous capacity for development, it is possible that they have tremendous gifts in art or cultural activities. Endowed with a keen critical sense, they will be great in business organisations.

Contrary Angel: Dominates selfishness, anger, hatred, hypocrisy and revenge. A person influenced by this contrary angel may be prone to sudden passion or infidelity. They may be presumptuous to plan retaliation and revenge or practice black magic.

Hierarchy: Principalities
Archangel: Aniel
Planet: Mercury
Power number: 3
Month of Change: March
Is present on Earth: from 16:00pm to 16:20pm
Incense: Mint
Colour of Candle: White
Weekday: Tuesday
Crystal: Coral
Psalm: 144, verse 3

"LORD, what is man, that thou take knowledge of him! Or the son of man, that thou make account of him!"

VEHUIAH

Protects days: 06/01 - 20/03 - 01/06 - 13/08 - 25/10

Invoke this angel to undertake and perform the most difficult things.

Influence: Those born under Vehuiah's influence are extremely curious and always in search of truth. They are balanced on the inside and have the gift of healing in their hands. Their angel protects the astral plane, causing them to take an interest in several subjects. They tend to find many lovers, but take time to disconnect from an old love. They face everything with optimism because of the nobility of their character in relation to friends. They love to see their family united at all times.

Professionally: Anyone born under this angel's protection is gifted with a shrewd and subtle spirit and will perform the most difficult tasks. They have the ability to learn about science and the arts. Inventive and creative, they are inspired artists. They are the precursor to a new world. People under Vehuiah's influence have the ability to write or speak with a penchant for politics. They have good manners and their work will be rewarded and recognized. They like competitions and try to break all records. They believe that difficult times enable spiritual growth. They love social life and possess strong magnetism and charisma, which could open doors to high society.

Contrary Angel: Influences turbulent people, fiery and choleric tempers. The angel dominates extravagance, gaffes, intellectual aggression; revenge, dramatic scenes and a strong sexual drive.

Hierarchy: Seraphim
Archangel: Metatron
Planet: Mars
Power number: 8
Month of Change: August
Weekday: 3rd Thursday of every month
Is present on Earth: from 0:05am - 0:20am
Colour of Candle: Yellow
Crystal: Ruby
Incense: Orange Blossom or Lavender
Psalm: 3, verse 4

"I cried unto the LORD with my voice, and he heard me out of his holy hill. Selah."

VEULIAH
Protects days: 17/02 - 01/05 - 13/07 - 24/09 - 06/12

Invoke this angel to destroy the forces of the enemy and free slaves, depressed people or people with addictions. Veuliah influences the prosperity of businesses and strengthens those who occupy a prominent position.

Influence: Those born under this angel's influence tend to have a healthy behaviour. They will be famous for their work, winning the confidence of society with their services. Veuliah's influence is noticeable among the most famous and powerful as it gives glory and prestige to them. Anyone under its protection uses modern ideas and strategic actions to improve their work and consolidate their position. They will always act with caution, avoiding obstacles, using common sense and intelligence to tackle problems. They carefully observe every path before taking the first step. Their accumulation of knowledge is acquired through hard work, to the extent only a privileged mind could develop throughout life. Those born under Veuliah's influence will be noble, sincere and unselfish in their relationships, enlightening all with their inexhaustible energy. They conquer their own space, their self-confidence and good humour, never wasting energy on inner conflicts.

Professionally: Anyone born under this angel's influence can be successful as a business professional, politician, and scientist or in any activity related to medicine.

Research would also be an appropriate choice as their patience could lead them to great discoveries.

Contrary Angel: Dominates discord between employers and employees or between partners, destruction of businesses, ruin, disaster, accidents, insatiable appetite, boundless egotism, bigotry, intrigues and bad advice.

Hierarchy: Virtues
Archangel: Raphael
Planet: Mars
Power number: 12
Month of Change: Decamber
Is present on Earth: from 14:00pm to 14:20 pm
Incense: Benzoin
Colour of Candle: Pale Blue
Weekday: Tuesday
Crystal: Hematite
Psalm: 87, verse 2 and 3

"The LORD loves the gates of Zion more than all the dwellings of Jacob. Glorious things are spoken of thee, O city of God. Selah."

YABAMIAH

Protects days: 16/03 - 28/05 - 09/08 - 21/10 - 02/01

This angel dominates interrelationships between generations and all phenomena of nature. Yabamiah protects those who regenerate or redeem through harmony, praising God and purifying the elementals. This angel also helps recover drugged and drunken people.

Influence: Those born under the influence of Yabamiah will be awarded with the power of the angelic world. They can regenerate people, plants or animals. Their confidence will always be contagious as their optimism in all areas of life: emotionally, socially and professionally. They are introspective and a little reserved at times, but see everything around them and when needed go into action immediately. They maintain their unwavering strength of character and great supremacy at any cost. Their image is in integrity and they will never have anything to hide. People born under Yabamiah's protection are very spiritual and detached from everything that is not essential. Their religion is truth and they search far to find it. They are true liberals. They may be knowledgeable of cosmic constellations, always receiving the information intuitively, constantly improving their knowledge with each new reading through their third eye. They are the owners of their destiny and do everything for destiny to run its course.

Professionally: Those born under the influence of this angel have a tendency for activities related to humanities, teaching and esotericism. They may be awarded in literature or philosophy.

Contrary Angel: Dominates atheism, criticism, controversy, literary dispute, dangerous writings, artificiality, futility, limitation, immaturity, incompetence, speculation and self-destruction.

Hierarchy: Angels
Archangel: Gabriel
Planet: Sun
Power number: 4
Month of Change: April
Is present on Earth: from 23:00pm to 23:20 pm
Incense: Benzoin
Colour of Candle: Lilac
Weekday: Friday
Crystal: Amethyst
Psalm: 91 verse 1 and 2

"He that dwelled in the secret place of the most high shall abide under the shadow of the Almighty. I will say of the LORD, He is my refuge and my fortress: my God; in him will I trust."

YELAIAH
Protects days: 18/02 - 02/05 - 14/07 - 25/09 - 12/07

Invoke this angel to help win legal proceedings and obtain protection from judges. Yelaiah protects against assaults and the dangers of edged weapons or firearms.

Influence: Those born under the influence of this angel will love to travel, are intelligent and all their ventures will succeed. They will be celebrated for their talent, courage and achievements. They will fight to keep traditions alive and preserve the memories of things dear to their heart. Travellers and researchers of historical facts, they will clarify any doubts or inconsistencies in this lifetime through memories of their previous lifetimes. They will promote cultural images that offer people historical content as well as natural beauty to enrich their wisdom. Generous at work, they always give opportunities to all, believing that great achievements are only attained through work. Someone under Yelaiah's protection is never dominated by discouragement and nothing will prevent them from achieving their goals. They will be safe, skilled and never risk their name and reputation in suspicious attitudes, letting life unfold spontaneously. They know how to manage their earnings, are safe and smart in their investments and never venture into something that has not yet unfolded. They always express their love in a constructive way and have the need to defend their dreams, whether related to their family, neighbourhood or cultural values. They will be respected, admired and able to find solutions to all problems. They are always creating ways to enhance the intellect of society. They are the pure inspiration of an angelic being.

Professionally: Those born under Yelaiah's influence can succeed as historians, anthropologists, sociologists, missionaries or in any activity related to humanities.

Contrary Angel: A person dominated by this contrary angel may cause misery in families, strife or war. They may be indifferent to the suffering of the humble, worship pagan gods, make people prisoners of toxicity, violate peace treaties or massacre prisoners without mercy.

Hierarchy: Virtues
Archangel: Raphael
Planet: Mercury
Power number: 6
Month of Change: June
Is present on Earth: from 14:20pm to 14:40 pm
Incense: Fennel
Colour of Candle: White
Weekday: Saturday
Crystal: Agate
Psalm: 118, verse 19

"Open to me the gates of righteousness: I will go into them, and I will praise the LORD."

YESALEL

Protects days: 18/01 - 01/04 - 13/06 - 25/08 - 06/11

Invoke this angel to assist with friendships and marital happiness. Yesalel helps provide easy understanding of all situations.

Influence: Those born under this angel's influence have a prodigious memory, a perfect and great intellectual capacity to understand everything in a logical manner, including the mystical or spiritual affairs. They always strive for the unity of the family, preserving fidelity. They will be faithful in showing love to one person. People under Yesalel's protection produce major reconciliations between people and are famous and known for their work. They have ideas about community work, linked to the creation of institutions to defend the family. Their great ability to accept life as it is, without complaining about anything, means they will always be surrounded by friends, whom they understand and never judge. They will have a deep knowledge of themselves and are great philosophers. Their spiritual body works in perfect harmony.

Professionally: Someone born under Yesalel's influence can be successful as a marriage counsellor or lawyer specialising in matrimonial cases. They are active participants in companies related to leisure or cultural associations.

Contrary Angel: Masters inconsistency, caprice, tyranny, deceit, coldness, ignorance and error. A person under the influence of this contrary angel may have a limited spirit and may laugh at people who are learning and writing about subjects they know only superficially. They are happy to see separated couples and disunity of the family

Hierarchy: Cherubim
Archangel: Haziel
Planet: Saturn
Power number: 7
Month of Change: June
Is present on Earth: from 04:00am to 04:20am
Incense: Mint
Colour of Candle: Baby Pink
Weekday: Saturday
Crystal: Rose Quartz
Psalm: 97, verse 1

"The LORD reigneth; let the earth rejoice; let the multitude of isles be glad thereof."

Angelic Help

Part 4

CHAPTER ELEVEN

An Angel for every situation - A to Z of angels to guide you

There are many angels and archangels. In conjunction with general roles as mentioned in other chapters, some of them have specific areas of responsibility or skills. Whatever challenge you may have, any opportunity you would like to enhance or any scenario or area of life and spiritual development you wish to progress, there will be a relevant angel or archangel you can call upon to assist or connect with.

Use the following to look up a relevant angel/archangel, and then invoke themas described in Chapters Six and Seven.

Remember to come back to refer to the list regularly!

A
Abundance - Zadkiel (Zad-kee-el) and Tubiel (Too-bee-el)
Acceptance - Ananchel (An-an-kel)
Animals, help for - Hariel (Har-ee-el)
Anger management - Phaleg (Far-leg)
Artistic inspiration - Radueriel (Rad-oo-ayr-iel
Awareness - Zephon (Zeff-on)

B
Beauty - Haniel (Han-ee-el)
Birds (tame) - Tubiel (Too-bee-el)

Birds (wild) - Anpiel (An-pee-el)
Blue Star, Angel of the - Sanusemi (San-oo-sem-ee)
Broken heart - Mupiel (Moo-pee-el)

C

Calculating risks - Barakiel (Bar-ak-ee-el)
Calming emotions - Phuel (Foo-el)
Celestial secrets - Raziel (Raz-ee-el)
Central Sun of All Central Suns (Sacred Heart of God/Universe)
Change of direction - Nadiel (Nad-ee-el)
Choices - Tabris (Tab-reez)
Clarifying issues - Ramiel (Ram-ee-el)
Cleansing life - Torquaret (Tork-ah-rett)
Climax of a matter - Amnediel (Am-ned-ee-el)
Closure on a matter - Geliel (Gel-ee-el)
Comfort - Rachmiel (Rak-mee-el) or Cassiel (Kass-ee-el)
Communication (written) - Dabriel (Dab-ree-el)
Communication (verbal) - Michael (Mik-ay-el)
Compassion - Rachmiel (Rak-mee-el) or Cassiel (Kass-ee-el)
Creativity - Uriel and Radueriel (Rad-oo-ayr-iel
Crystals, power of - Och (Ok)
Confidence in leadership - Verchiel (Ver-kee-el)
Cosmic Spirit (Essence of the Stars) - Seraphiel (Ser-af-ee-el)
Courage and confidence - Camael (Kam-ay-el)

D

Decisions - Zuriel (Zoo-ree-el)
De-cluttering your life - Tual (Too-al)
Deliverance from a situation - Pedael (Ped-ay-el)
Destiny, seeking - Oriel (Oo-ree-el)

Divine connection - Metatron/Shekinah (Met-at-ron)
(Shek-ee-nah)
Door to Light - Tabris (Tab-reez)
Dreams and hopes - Gabriel (Gab-ree-el)

Ӕ

Emotional calm - Phuel (Foo-el)
Empowerment - Camael (Kam-ay-el)
Energy and wellbeing - Mumiah (Moo-mee-ah)
Expansion of personal horizons - Adnachiel (Ad-nak-ee-el)
Exploration - Elemiah (El-em-eye-ah)

Ϝ

Faithfulness and loyalty - Icabel (Ik-ah-bel)
Fertility of body - Yusamin (Yoo-sam-een)
Fertility of mind (new ideas) - Yusamin (Yoo-sam-een)
Financial affairs - Vasariah (Vass-ah-ree-ah)
Finding lost things/self - Rochel (Rosh-el)
Flower secrets - Achaiah (Ak-ay-ah) and Anahita (Ana-hee-tah)
Food and nourishment - Isda (Iz-dah)
Forgiving/atoning for the past - Phanuel (Fan-oo-el)
Free will/choices - Tabris (Tab-reez)
Future harmony - Isiaiel (Iz-ay-el)

Ӈ

Harmony - Cassiel (Kass-ee-el) and Raphael (Raf-ay-el)
Healing, general - Raphael (Raf-ay-el)
Healing of sun - Raphael (Raf-ay-el) and Savatri (Sav-at-ree)
Healing plants - Anahita (Ana-hee-tah)
Healing the past - Phanuel (Fan-oo-el)

Health and wholeness - Sofiel (Sof-ee-el)
Heartbreak - Mupiel (Moo-pee-el)
Heart's desire - Pagiel (Pagg-ee-el)
Heavenly peace - Anafiel (Ana-fee-el)
Hidden talents - Parasiel (Para-see-el)
Home/work balance - Dokiel (Dok-ee-el)
Home/work relationships - Hamaliel (Hama-lee-el)
Hopes and dreams - Gabriel (Gab-ree-el)
Hurts - Matriel (Mat-ree-el)

G

Goals in life - Machidiel (Mak-id-ee-el) or Gabriel (Gab-ree-el)
Going with the flow - Haurvatat (Hoor-vat-at)
Good luck (golden) - Diniel (Din-ee-el) and Kadmiel (Kad-mee-el)
Good luck (silver) - Aniel (An-ee-el) and Padiel (Pad-ee-el)
Golden protection - Diniel (Din-ee-el) and Kadmiel (Kad-mee-el)
Graceful acceptance - Ananchel (An-an-kel)

I

Ideas, new - Yusamin (Yoo-sam-een), Spugliguel (Spug-ligg-oo-el)
Inner feelings - Muriel (Moo-ree-el)
Innovation - Uriel (Oor-ee-el)
Insight - Zikiel (Zik-ee-el)
Inspiration, artistic - Radueriel (Rad-oo-ayr-iel
Inspiration, flash of - Zikiel (Zik-ee-el)
Inspiration, music - Tagas (Tag-az)
Inspiration, poetry - Israfel (Iz-raf-el)
Intuitive problem-solving - Ambriel (Am-bree-el)

Intuitive skills - Cambiel (Kam-bee-el) and Ofaniel (Off-an-ee-el)
Invisibility - Aniel (An-ee-el) and Padiel (Pad-ee-el)

J

Jobs/roles in life - Jofiel (Joff-ee-el)
Joy - Haniel (Han-ee-el) and Zadkiel (Zad-kee-el)

K

Kindness - Zadkiel (Zad-kee-el)
Key to Heavenly Peace - Anafiel (Ana-fee-el)

L

Leadership - Verchiel (Ver-kee-el)
Life partners - Shekinah (Shek-ee-nah)
Living your truth - Michael (Mik-ay-el)
Lost things - Rochel (Rosh-el)
Love, self-confidence - Haniel (Han-ee-el)
Love, power of - Rikbiel (Rik-bee-el)
Love, sexual - Rachiel (Rak-ee-el)
Loving kindness - Amabiel (Ama-bee-el)
Loving relationships - Haniel (Han-ee-el), Shekinah (Shek-ee-nah), Amabiel (Ama-bee-el)
Loyalty and faithfulness - Icabel (Ik-ah-bel)

M

Magic of nature - Aratron (Ar-at-ron)
Managing time - Eth (Eth)
Metals, power of - Hagith (Hag-ith)
Moon power - Cambiel (Kam-bee-el), Ofaniel (Off-an-ee-el), Geniel (Gen-ee-el), Amnediel (Am-ned-ee-el), Adiel (Ad-ee-el), Geliel (Gel-ee-el)

Moons, two - Mirabiel (Mee-rah-bee-el)
Mountains and peace - Rampel (Ram-pel)
Moving house or country - Nadiel (Nad-ee-el)
Music and harmony - Tagas (Tag-az)

N

Nature's secrets - Achaiah (Ak-ay-ah)
Nature's magic - Aratron (Ar-at-ron)
Nature's plants and peace - Sachluph (Sak-luff)
New plans - Spugliguel
New projects (calculation of risks) - Barakiel (Bar-ak-ee-el)
New project commencement - Geniel (Gen-ee-el)

O

Opportunity for abundance - Tubiel (Too-bee-el)

P

Passion for life - Nathaniel (Nath-an-ee-el)
Patience - Achaiah (Ak-ay-ah), Michael (Mik-ay-el), Rampel (Ram-pel)
Peace with nature - Sachluph (Sak-luff) and Zuphlas (Zoof-laz)
Personal beliefs - Arad (Ar-ad)
Personal vision and expansion - Adnachiel (Ad-nak-ee-el)
Philosophy and wisdom - Hermes Trismegistus (Her-meez Triz-mej-istus)
Pitfalls - Zephon (Zef-on)
Poetry - Israfel (Iz-raf-el)
Power of will and mind - Gazardiel (Gaz-ahd-ee-el)
Prayer, power of - Sandalphon (San-dal-fon)
Problem-solving - Ambriel (Am-bree-el)

Protection, general - Michael (Mik-ay-el)
Psychic awareness - Barakiel (Bar-ak-ee-el)
Psychic/spiritual development - Aratron (Ar-at-ron) or
Ariel (A-ree-el)

Q

Quiet reflection/inner still point - Duma (Doo-mah)

R

Rainbows, power of - Hahlii (Hah-lee-eye)
Reach for the sky - Sahaqiel (Sah-hak-ee-el)
Recuperation and rest - Farlas (Far-laz)
Re-launch your future - Spugliguel (Spug-ligg-oo-el)
Re-programme life template - Pistis Sophia (Pis-tis-Sof-
ee-ah)
Right job or role - Jofiel (Jof-fee-el)
Rivers - Haurvatat (Hoor-vat-at)

S

Sea mammals - Manakel (Man-ak-el)
Secret wisdom - Raziel (Raz-ee-el) and Hermes
Trismegistus (Her-meez Triz-mej-istus)
Seeking something - Salathiel (Sal-ath-ee-el)
Self-belief - Arad (Ar-ad), Haniel (Han-ee-el) or Pistis
Sophia (Pis-tis-Sof-ee-ah)
Sensitivity - Barakiel (Bar-ak-ee-el)
Serenity - Cassiel (Kass-ee-el)
Sexuality - Amabiel (Amah-bee-el)
Silent reflection - Duma (Doo-mah)
Silver protection - Aniel (An-ee-el) and Padiel (Pad-ee-
el)
Simplify life - Tual (Too-al)

Sky's the limit - Sahaqiel (Sah-ak-ee-el)
Source (healing) - Seraphiel (Ser-af-ee-el)
Speaking your truth - Michael (Mik-ay-el)
Spiritual development - Ariel (A-ree-el), Melchisadec (Mel-kee-zad-ek), Metatron (Met-at-ron)
Spiritual fulfilment - Melchisadec (Mel-kee-zad-ek)
Strength - Michael (Mik-ay-el) or Zeruch (Zer-ook)

T

Taking stock - Torquaret (Tork-ah-rett)
Tranquillity - Phuel (Foo-el)
Transformation - Uriel (Oor-ee-el)
Trees, peacefulness - Zuphlas (Zoof-laz)
True love - Amabiel (Am-ah-bee-el)
True self - Ithuriel (Ith-oo-ree-el)
Truth - Michael (Mik-ay-el)

V

Vision (new) - Adnachiel (Ad-nak-ee-el)
Voicing inner feelings - Muriel (Moo-ree-el)

W

Washing away hurts - Matriel (Mat-ree-el)
Wellbeing and energy - Mumiah (Moo-mee-ah)
Wholeness and health - Sofiel (Sof-ee-el)
Wild animals and birds - Thuriel (Thur-ee-el)) and Anpiel (An-pee-el)
Willpower - Gazardiel (Gaz-ah-dee-el), Raphael (Raf-ay-el)
Winds of change - Ruhiel (Roo-hee-el)
Winding down situations - Adiel (Ad-ee-el)
Wisdom - Zadkiel (Zad-kee-el)
Work/home balance - Dokiel (Dok-ee-el)

Work/home relationships - Hamaliel (Hama-lee-el)
Worries - Iadiel (Ee-ah-dee-el)

CHAPTER TWELVE

Angels to call when you need immediate help

Spiritual, Emotional and Physical Protection - Archangel Michael

Call upon Archangel Michael when you need:

⊙ Protection, strength and empowerment, help with overcoming fears and negative emotions. Removal of all kinds of harmful and toxic negative energy and psychic attacks

⊙ To let go of grief, sadness, emotional pain and sorrow deeply embedded in your heart

Spiritual Healing - Archangel Zadkiel

⊙ Call upon Archangel Zadkiel to bring you more spiritual discernment and wisdom

⊙ He will help you clear your mind so you will be able to better comprehend and understand your surroundings

⊙ He will help with emotional/physical detachment and letting go of what is no longer in your highest good

⊙ He will help you release all painful and emotional blockages and deep memories, bringing you to a place of peace and safety.

Emotional and Spiritual Healing - Archangel Chamuel

Call upon Archangel Chamuel to assist you when:

◎　　You need to bring love into your heart and to help you feel pure unconditional divine love

◎　　You need to let go of deep pain from the past, restore your heart to full health by bringing the innocence and feelings of compassion to your heart chakra once again.

◎　　You need to let go of feelings of judgement by you and towards others.

◎　　You need to move from your analytical head space to being heart centred, and use your heart and your intuition to move and flow in your river of life.

Physical, Emotional and Spiritual Healing - Archangel Raphael

◎　　Archangel Raphael is known to be the "Master Healer" of all Archangels

◎　　Call upon Archangel Raphael to help you and support you in the healing process of yourself and of others

◎　　Ask assistance when you need healing on a physical, spiritual and emotional level

◎　　Call him to cut spiritual and emotional chords and imagine a laser beam of emerald loving healing light being directed at the severed chords, both yours and the other persons.

Education, Exams - Archangel Jophiel and the Angels of Illumination

⊘ Call upon Archangel Jophiel when you or your loved ones need help with study and exams

Romance - Archangel Chamuel and the Angels of Love

⊘ Helps you with finding your true Love, your Twin Flame (the other half of you)
⊘ Helps you with relationship/emotional healing
⊘ Helps with the nurturing of pure unconditional love

Childbirth - Archangel Gabriel and the assisting angels Armisael - Angel of the womb, Temeluch - protector of children at birth and throughout their childhood

⊘ Helps with all things to do with childbirth and midwives
⊘ Helps relieving pain during labour
⊘ Helps having harmony and pure bliss on the labour ward

Departure or Transition of a Soul - Archangel Gabriel and the 'shepherding' Angels

⊘ Helps guiding the departing soul on the three days of their transitional journey (when a soul leaves the physical body)
⊘ Call upon these Angels for emotional support for the soul and also for the loved ones left behind: **Suriel,**

Cassiel, Azrael, Kafziel, Metatron, Yehudiah and Michael

๑   For help with the departure or transition of animals and pets call upon **Angel Meshabber**

Bereavement - Angel Yehudiah (beneficial Angel of Death) and the "releasing angels"

๑   These Angels ensure that the soul is carried away to its final destination

Call upon them when:

๑   Someone is about to pass over to the spiritual plane, when praying after the loss of a loved one.
๑   When praying each year on their birthday or on dates that are significant
๑   When remembering the day of their passing.

CHAPTER THIRTEEN

Your Astrological Angel

Some specific Angels and Archangels are connected to particular star signs as are some of the planets. They will influence people that are born under their protection in a very positive way. All the Angels that rule the astrological signs focus their work on our centre of emotions, our heart. They will bring out the best in us, in a very positive manner, taking us back to the divine source of unconditional love, so it is important that you invoke your star sign Angel or Archangel, especially during the month of your birthday - to complement your astrological characteristics ruled by your planets.

Aries
March 21 to April 19

Samuel is the Angel that protects people born under this star sign.

He will give you the strength to manage all things related to your heart, facilitating a calm and peaceful way of dealing with your emotions and more loving relationships. You will be helped in calming down, for example any wild emotions.
Incense: Violet

Taurus
April 22 to May 20

Anael is the Angel that protects people born under at this star sign.

Angel Anael will bring you high positive vibrations. Also, most importantly, you will be helped with all issues related to your love life, bringing out your charm and taming any needs for control with regards to your most deep emotions, thus balancing and harmonising you.
Incense: Verbena

Gemini
May 21 to June 20

Archangel Raphael is the Angel that protects people born under this star sign.

Archangel Raphael is the Master Healer and as a healer he will bring equilibrium, harmony, and health to all areas of your life but most specifically to your feelings and deeply embedded emotions, helping you peel away any layers of pain.
Incense: Lavender

Cancer
June 21 to July 22

Archangel Gabriel is the Angel that protects people born under this star sign.

Archangel Gabriel is renowned for taking care of the matters of the heart. He will ensure that you will not sustain adverse effects on your heart as people ruled by this star sign are extremely sensitive emotionally. He will bring you balance and will bring streams of positive energy so that you are able to cope with any obstacles that presents themselves to you in your life path. Gabriel will also ensure that you are emotionally centred and in full control of your emotions.

Incense: Jasmine

Leo
July 23 to August 22

Archangel Michael is the Angel that protects people born under this star sign.

Archangel Michael is a protector; he will protect you from all kinds of negative toxic energies, emotions and he will empower you to bring your own power and magnetic force to the surface. He will ensure that you are on the right path helping you have high levels of awareness and wisdom.

Incense: Myrrh

Virgo
August 23 to September 22

Archangel Raphael is the Angel that protects people born under this star sign.

Archangel Raphael is the Master Healer and as a healer will bring equilibrium, harmony, and health to all areas of your life but most specifically to your inner feelings and emotions. Specifically for Virgos, Raphael will also help with those that are extremely shy by bringing out their charisma and self-esteem.

Incense: Patchouli

Libra
September 23 to October 22

Anael is the Angel that protects people born under this star sign.

Anael will always bring you high positive energetic vibrations. Most importantly, this Archangel will help you with all issues related to love life and relationships, bringing your charisma and at times charm to the fore, by taming down your need for control related to your deepest emotions and fears. He will balance and harmonise you at a deeper level, creating the perfect conditions so you are able to experience true unconditional divine love.

Incense: Jasmine

Scorpio
October 23 to November 21

Azael is the Angel that protects people born under this star sign.

Azael will bring much love and divine light into your heart, mind, and especially into your thoughts. Azael will bring out in you the true power of positive thinking; showing you how to see the light in the end of the tunnel, and a new door when another is closed. This will attract many people into your life as you are a tool to help them, being an example to many.

Incense: Violet

Sagittarius
November 22th to December 21th

Saquiel is the Angel that protects people born under this star sign.

Saquiel will bring you positive emotions and bursts of energy, especially in matters related to the heart. He will help you in a very strong and positive way in times of disputes and misunderstandings, bringing peace, truth and harmony. Above all he will bring sympathy, happiness and joy when people are around you.
Incense: Peppermint

Capricorn
December 22 to January 19

Cassiel is the Angel that protects people born under this star sign.

Cassiel will be with you in every moment in every thought bringing out your intuition in a very positive way and showing you new paths and doorways to your true higher self. He will bring you closer to the ones you love by reigniting true unconditional divine love in your heart.
Incense: Violet

Aquarius
January 20 to February 18

Archangel Uriel is the Angel that protects people born under this star sign.

Archangel Uriel will bring you tremendous and amazing inner peace, love and tranquillity in your love life. He will bring out your inner power, self-esteem and

charisma so that you may shine with a pure loving divine heart in all areas of your life. This will make a major impact on the lives of people that you interact with.
Incense: Fennel

Pisces
February 19 to March 20

Asariel is the Angel that protects people born under this star sign.

Asariel will have a very important role in your love and social life bringing out the best of your emotions, happiness, enthusiasm, joy and fulfilment. This will leave people wanting to be around your energy all the time, so please bear in mind the need to protect yourself energetically at all times, as people may use the opportunity to 'suck you dry', energetically speaking.
Incense: Musk

CHAPTER FOURTEEN

Chakras and Angels

Chakras are energy centres within and above and below the human body. Our chakra system is also ruled by specific angels, where they can assist you in keeping your chakras in perfect harmony and health. When doing your meditations/visualisations, ask the angels to clear away all blocks in your chakras and to restore them to perfect energy flow and balance.

Invoke the angel in charge of the chakra that you need to work on and you will truly see the difference in your levels of energy. Working with the Angels when you are working on your chakras will increase your energy level immensely and above all you will feel deeply the joy, harmony, unconditional divine love and pure peace in your heart that you are only able to feel fully when you work with beings of such high energy vibration. You will also feel a major improvement in your intuition and enthusiasm when you let angels support you during work on your chakras.

If it is the first time you are working with angels to aid you with your chakras, I suggest you start gently with the first chakra and work on that one for at least a week before you move on to the next one. When you are comfortable and used to the presence of angels, then move on to the next stage of doing all the chakras. It's important that you take your time, just like doing a new exercise, and the more you do it the better you will get at it.

Chakras and Archangels

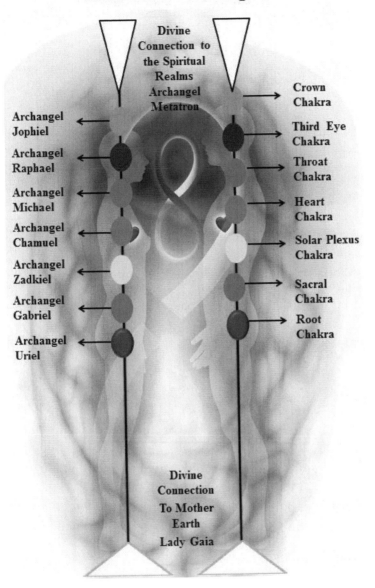

Divine
Connection to
the Spiritual
Realms
Archangel
Metatron

Crown
Chakra

Archangel
Jophiel

Third Eye
Chakra

Archangel
Raphael

Throat
Chakra

Archangel
Michael

Heart
Chakra

Archangel
Chamuel

Solar Plexus
Chakra

Archangel
Zadkiel

Sacral
Chakra

Archangel
Gabriel

Root
Chakra

Archangel
Uriel

Divine
Connection
To Mother
Earth
Lady Gaia

Root or Base Chakra
(Crystalline Red)
Base of spine
Chakra of Consciousness and Unconsciousness

Angel in charge: Archangel Uriel (pronounced yur-i-el), Angel of Peace.

Colour: Crystalline Red (when in perfect balance and health)

Ask the angel for: inner peace, untangling anger and fear from your heart, also to renew your hope, trust and faith. Ask Archangel Uriel to assist you when you need a peaceful resolution regarding issues with relationships. This Archangel also helps ending wars and disturbances in the world, promoting brotherhood and understanding.

Sacral Chakra
(Crystalline Orange)
Above the pelvis
Chakra of Power and Weakness

Angel in charge: Archangel Gabriel (pronounced ga-bri-el), Angel of Guidance.

Colour when angel is working: Emerald Green

Ask the angel for: revealing your life purpose and to give guidance in the right direction. Archangel Gabriel will also assist you in establishing discipline, order and balance in your life. This archangel helps aid organisations delivering and distributing food and medical assistance with integrity.

Solar Plexus Chakra
(Crystalline Yellow)
Stomach Area
Chakra of Joy and Sadness

Angel in charge: Archangel Zadkiel (pronounced zad-ki-el), Angel of Joy.

Colour when angel is working: Yellow

Ask the angel for: forgiveness, justice, mercy, joy, happiness, tolerance, and diplomacy, inspiration (especially for scientists, architects, designers and actors). Also ask for Archangel Zadkiel for help in removing all memories of strife among nations so all can work together in harmony.

Heart Chakra
(Crystalline Green)
Heart Area
Chakra of Love and Fear

Angel in charge: Archangel Chamuel (pronounced cha-mu-el), Angel of Love.

Colour when angel is working: Pink

Ask the angel for: Enhancement of your spiritual gifts, such as unconditional divine love, compassion, mercy for your fellow man. You can also ask this angel for assistance in repairing broken and damaged relationships. This angel will also help healing racial and ethnic tension.

Throat Chakra
(Crystalline Blue)
Neck and Throat Area
Chakra of peace, balance, harmony, freedom of
expression and anger

Angel in charge: Archangel Michael - (pronounced mic-i-el), Angel of Protection.

Colour when angel is working: Purple and gold.

Ask the angel for: freedom from doubt and fear; protection from physical and spiritual harm.

Third Eye Chakra
(Crystalline Indigo)
Forehead Area (middle of the eyebrows)

Chakra of intuition, guidance and pain

Angel in charge: Archangel Raphael (pronounced ra-phi-el), Angel of Healing.

Colour when angel is working: White

Ask the angel for: wholeness, vision, and spiritual sight, inspiration, healing of your mind, body, soul and spirit. You can also ask him to help in find new cures for illness.

Crown Chakra
(Crystalline Violet)
Top of the Head
Chakra of wisdom, enthusiasm and analytic thinking

Angel in charge: Jophiel (pronounced jo-fi-el), Angel of Illumination.

Colour when angel is working: Yellow/Gold

Ask the angel for: wisdom, illumination, understanding, inspiration, knowledge, clear thinking/seeing, and a deeper connection with your Higher Self. This Archangel also helps energetically cleaning our planet by freeing people from all types of addictions (physical and spiritual) and narrow-mindedness.

CHAPTER FIFTEEN

Cleanse your Home with Angelic help

The presence of the Angels generally and in the home is very subtle, and similarly the presence of the contrary Angel can also be, manifesting itself for example in misunderstandings and lack of harmony between the people who coexist in the same house. If you are experiencing this situation, there is a very simple way to move these negative energies and influences away.

Write the names of all the Guardian Angels of the people who live in the house in an invisible form, this means symbolically, in the frame of your front door. For example, you can "write" in the air with your finger, then in each bedroom, "write" in every corner of the room, the name of the Guardian Angel of the person that sleeps in the rooms. As you do this, say the following prayer:

"Each house has a corner, every corner has an angel, in the name of the Father, of the Son and the Holy Spirit, amen"

In the other rooms of the house, "write" the name of your own Guardian Angel.

Also generally share any concerns with the others sharing the household, demonstrate a loving attitude and without doubt, this way you contribute to a harmonious home life and will be better prepared to receive the gifts from the angelic world.

CHAPTER SIXTEEN

Clearing Your Heart meditation with angelic help

Go to a calm place, away from distractions.

Relax your body and mind.

Inhale deeply, and whilst doing this bring the angelic energies of God to you. Hold your breath for a little while.

Then exhale, letting go of all negative energies and feelings, tensions, worries, anger and anxiety.

As you do this, ask for all of that to be transmuted into positive energies.

Do this as many times as you need to, until you can feel positive energy flowing through your body.

Visualize yourself filled with a strong bright loving white light.

Love that light, glorify the light, give yourself gently to the presence of God and decree (say):

"I am the presence of God in action.
I am the flame of the Trinity of this heart, which is inundated with Love, Wisdom and Power.
I am an open door that no one can close

I AM How I AM! "

Visualize the colours pink, yellow and blue in your heart, and make them shiny. These are the colours of the Holy Trinity, the colours of healing.

CHAPTER SEVENTEEN

Prayer for the Angels of Healing and Protection

"May the angels bless me with divine protection. May the healing love of the angels surround me wherever I go. I ask that I may be a vehicle for spiritual healing. I ask that I may receive angelic healing on a daily basis. My spirit is constantly healed by ministering angels. My guardian angel always guides me to the healers, doctors, and therapists that can best help me. I thank my angels for their transformative influence upon my soul. I ask that I may learn to heal myself, become more positive, and evolve spiritually. I ask that I may bless the lives of others with the healing and protection of the angels."

CHAPTER EIGHTEEN

Contrary angel

Have you ever felt very irritated by silly little things?

How many times have you got involved in an argument for no apparent reason?

How many times have you felt anxious for no reason? Have you ever noticed that your behaviour is curt, surly or rude, and your words full of anger and hatred towards someone you love who doesn't deserve it?

Have you felt that, you can't explain why/what caused you to behave like that?

The cause of all this could have been the contrary angel taking advantage of a moment of carelessness, a lack of vigilance on your part. Stop and ask yourself whether this is the first time it has happened.

Notice how the negative influence of the contrary angel is very is similar to your own essence.

In every ordinary interaction with another person there is a competing, opposing force which we are rarely aware of. This can happen without us noticing because we interact with so many people every day, and it's difficult to recognise the contrary angel when it is present.
The way to prevent the contrary angel from wreaking havoc in your life is to break down what is not necessary in you. Remove any layers of insecurities, the 'onion

layers', the unnecessary armour that is outdated and rusty and doesn't protect you properly anyway. Be mindful that when you shift something in you, the universe will send you an experience to test you! The attacks by the contrary angel will get stronger and stronger every time until you deal with the "onion layer" and shed it as unnecessary.

Here are some tips to help you spot the influence of the contrary angel in yourself and others around you.

There are five different situations to look out for:

Contrary angel in love relationships:

- Constant fighting without reasonable cause.
- Exaggerated jealousy for no reason.
- Lack of companionship with your loved one.
- Forgetting about important dates.
- Not taking care of your looks when going out with your loved one.
- Listening to idle gossip from people who lack credibility.
- Making the most of every opportunity to humiliate your loved one in front of others.
- Showing no interest whatsoever in what your loved one is saying or doing.
- Postponing a request from your loved one indefinitely.
- Excluding the loved one when talking to God/Goddess.

Contrary angel in relationships in general:

- Refusing to help a loved one in need.

- Betraying and deceiving friends.
- Attitudes of revenge with colleagues.
- Starting gossip and supporting gossip between people close to you.
- Negativity and envy towards the success of a person.
- Provoking fights between friends and then moving away from them.
- Manipulating someone to take advantage of their friendship.
- Giving more attention to one person than another.
- Treating friends with arrogance and contempt.

Contrary angel in professional relationships:

- Acting without integrity to damage work colleagues.
- Refusing to help a colleague who is overwhelmed with work.
- Being arrogant.
- Laughing at the misfortune of a colleague.
- Abusing power in the workplace.
- Bad mouthing and gossip.
- Doing anything which is illegal.
- Becoming revengeful and unjust.
- Not being able to hold a job for long.
- Manipulating or unreasonably assigning a colleague with your workload.
-

Contrary angel in family relationships:

- Messing up the house.
- Isolating and ignoring loved ones.
- Invading the privacy of loved ones.

- Keeping pain in the heart (as opposed to expressing it)
- Starting family fights and feuds
- Promoting discord among family members
- Refusing advice from elders.
- Mistreating siblings and parents
- Breakdown of family bonds
- Becoming vain and full of pride

Contrary angel in private life:

- Lack of faith in God/Goddess
- Becoming lazy
- Creating 'accidents'
- Not being able to study or concentrate for long periods of time.
- Feeling a strong attraction to alcoholic drinks
- Getting involved with any kind of forbidden drugs
- Abusing health
- Starting public scandals.

Contrary angel in your community:

- Nuisance neighbours
- Yobbish behaviour and intimidating groups taking over public spaces
- Vandalism, graffiti and fly-posting
- People dealing and buying drugs on the street
- People dumping rubbish and abandoning cars
- Begging and anti-social drinking
- The misuse of fireworks
- Reckless driving

Remove the influence of the contrary angel from your life by using your Guardian Angel as listed in Chapter Ten. By giving him or her light you can remove all the negativity from the contrary angel and let good manifest itself.

To restore spiritual equilibrium and inner peace, you need to have faith that all evil can be cast away.

You can do this by invoking your guardian angel to neutralise the vibration of the contrary angel. Make it a regular habit to dedicate a few minutes to the spiritual world as soon as you wake up in the morning.

Meditate quietly for a few minutes or say a prayer, such as Psalm 91, and follow this with your guardian angel's psalm and light a white candle. To complete the harmonious ambience, light your guardian angel's incense and walk through the house with it, allowing the aroma of the good spirit to waft around creating a positive atmosphere throughout your home.

The time when your guardian angel is around is the best time to light your candle and incense.

Carry a crystal around with you which corresponds with your guardian angel. This could be as earrings, chains, bracelets, pendants or simply in your wallet.

Working with Archangels

Part 5

CHAPTER NINETEEN

Using Archangel Prayers to enhance your life

Archangels and angels just love prayers, it is music to their ears. They rejoice when they hear our prayers, being prayers of gratitude, praise or when we need a little help to remove the obstacles out of our path. As I said before Archangels and angels are only able to assist us when we give them permission and assign them tasks, otherwise they will only stay around watching, as they are not allowed to interfere in our free will and choices.

Archangels can assist you in various tasks and areas of your life, but it is extremely important that all that you ask for is from a place of love, stripping away your ego, pride and what you think "you" want. This is where many people fail with their requests and then say that their prayers are not being answered. When the angelic world responds to a prayer or request is because it is for your highest good and orders have been sent from up above for them to do so there is a chain of command that cannot be overridden, so every time you turn to the angelic realms for help, open your heart wide and ask from a place of unconditional love, align your energy to your angels energy and see miracles happening. When working with such pure beings of divine light, all that you need is be your true self, have faith and above all trust that what you are asking - if it is for your highest good - will be delivered to you, sometimes even more then you asked for. If you see that your request is not coming to you, step back and ask your angel to show you the reason why. Many are the ones that ask but yet they are not ready to receive it. If this is the case, ask your angel to prepare you for it. If you are still not receiving your request then ask your angel to show you another solution, *as an Angel cannot help unless you ASK.* It is God's law that without human requisition, an Angel may not intervene in a human's affairs. All angels need express permission and consent, unless it is a life-threatening emergency and they have orders from higher up. You do not need to do any "rituals" to call the Angels, although some feel it helps them connect more easily. All you need is to ask and to have the intention. Believe that the Angels are with you and that they are there to help you with the issue you are facing. It's all so simple...be childlike!

Archangel Michael

This almighty Archangel is the Supreme Protector of all that relates to justice, honour and truth. He carries the sword of freedom in his right hand and the scales of justice in his left hand ensuring a perfect balance. Archangel Michael has a legion of blue-flamed angels at his service and they are given this name due to his majestic blue-flamed cloak. People often call upon his cloak for protection during meditation or spiritual development and also for protection of their homes and loved ones, especially children while they sleep.

Michael is known as a "multi-tasking" Archangel as he is not limited to one task alone, unlike the other Archangels who have specific tasks and missions. Archangel Michael is able to shift his energy when called upon, from helping you heal in all areas of your life, to cutting away cords, webs and strands of negativity that is clinging to you, to removing all entities and earth bound spirits in the environment around you and your loved ones. This is where his power and strength lies.

Almighty Archangel Michael is also very well known for being associated with the power of communication (spoken/written) and the Throat Chakra which governs the way we express ourselves to the world. He plays a very important role in our spiritual evolution, awakening and enlightenment. He serves as a gateway between our heart, the centre of all our soul emotions and our mind and the logical thinking. Archangel Michael is the peace maker, when called upon he will immediately bring a peaceful solution to arguments or disagreements that have occurred between family members, friends, and even complete strangers!

Astrological Sign: Leo
Ruling Day: Sunday
Chakra: Throat
Physical Associations: Throat, Thyroid, Mouth, Nose, Ears, Upper Respiratory
Crystals: Amber, Clear Quartz, Golden Topaz, Lapis Lazuli,
Essential Oils: Anise Star, Aniseed, Black Pepper, Cajuput, Carnation, Clary Sage, Clove, Cumin, Elemi, Frankincense, Galbanum, Geranium, Ginger, Hyssop, Juniper, Lavender, Lime, Melissa, Mimosa, Myrrh, Oak moss, Palma Rosa, Pimento Berry, Pine, Rosemary, Sage, Sweet Fennel, Tea-tree, Thyme, Valerian, Violet, Yarrow
Candle Colours: Sky blue to help with communication between planes of existence

Call upon Michael to assist you when:

 ⟡ You are in need of courage, strength and protection
 ⟡ You feel unsafe, verbally and physically attacked or abused
 ⟡ You need to protect your home, material belongings and work environment
 ⟡ You are doing any type of spiritual work or developing spiritually/psychically
 ⟡ You want to cut emotional cords, webs, and spiritual strands that `bind' you to any type of relationship

๑ You need guidance in a situation and see justice done by your name
๑ You need assistance clearing and removing of all negative energies from within and around you or you feel you are under a psychic attack.

Prayer to Archangel Michael:

"I call upon my dear beloved Archangel Michael. I ask that you come to me now with your army of blue-flamed angels. Almighty Archangel of light, give me strength and courage to see my day through, give me wisdom to live my life in truth and integrity always. Show me how to change my inner core so I let go deep in my heart of what no longer serves me. My dearest angel of light, protect me under your magnificent wings of blue light. Give me every day the courage and strength to resolve and experience all that comes my way so I'm able to grow, may the truth be always revealed when injustice is done by my name and the ones I see close to my heart. I am grateful for all that I have and all that will be given to me. I thank you deeply from my heart."

Archangel Gabriel

Archangel Gabriel communicates to us through our heart. Archangel is the "Bearer of God's good news" as the messenger of God. This powerful Archangel is the only female Archangel and she is there, waiting for you to ask for guidance. Allow yourself to feel her presence, and ask silently within your heart or out-loud if you so choose, for your heart's desire. Like a stream, the ideas will flow to you, allowing your unlimited potential to shine through in all glory! The name Gabriel means "God is my strength" and is known for being associated with the moon as it uses feminine intuitive energy to help clarifying dream interpretations and visions.

Astrological Sign: Gemini
Ruling Day: Monday
Chakra: Solar-plexus
Physical Associations: Lower abdomen, Stomach, Intestines, Ovaries, Bladder
Crystals: Moonstone, Aquamarine, Selenite, Citrine, Blue Lace Agate
Essential Oils: Angelica seed, Anise Star , Basil, Bay, Benzoin, Cinnamon, Clary Sage, Coriander, Dill seed , Elemi - Immortelle, Lemon Verbena, Linden Blossom, Melissa , Mimosa, Myrrh, Narcissus, Neroli, Rose, Spearmint
Candle Colours: Light Lavender or Pink to help you open up your heart.

Call upon Archangel Gabriel to assist you when:

☙ You are going through major life changing experiences and need to be guided to find and understand your mission and life purpose

☙ You need extra help cleansing away all fear-based emotional burdens through 'purification'

☙ You need help paying attention to your inner heart

☙ You need extra help in understanding angelic signs and synchronicities in your life

☙ You are overwhelmed and need to set yourself free of impure and negative thoughts

☙ Your home has toxic spiritual clutter or when you have absorbed other people's emotions and toxic energies

☙ You have been assaulted, emotionally, physically or sexually

Prayer to Archangel Gabriel

"I call upon you my dear beloved Archangel Gabriel, in the name of the most pure unconditional love and divine light, guide my heart, my soul and my spirit. Unveil to and guide me through my soul's true journey by revealing my true me and my true purpose in this life time. Guide me in the right direction and give me the ability to understand my dreams and visions that are sent from above, so that I can be truly be inspired and guided in the present, seeding for my future during my life changes. I ask you being humble in my heart, to help me to purify my body, mind, soul and spirit of all toxic substances and thoughts at all times. With my heart full of joy as I know you are already working

within my heart, I give you all my gratitude and thank you deeply from my heart."

Archangel Raphael

Archangel Raphael is commonly known throughout many religions as the Angel of Healing. His name means "God Heals". He is considered the Supreme Healer among all the Archangels, and he is also one of the Guardians of the Tree of Life.

When you call upon him, he is there instantly and is certainly not shy about letting his presence be known. You may notice sparkles of green, have goose bumps all over your body or a deep sense of calm coming over you. When you ask for Raphael's assistance, his loving energy automatically pervades the space around you and into you, affecting all involved positively.

Archangel Raphael brings to us the knowledge of self-healing and how to master it, by helping us realize that we are all healers. We just need to tap into that stream of energy, which can be done any time it is needed.

When working closely with Archangel Raphael you are overcome with the feeling of wanting to "Heal the World", as he brings to you the realisation that we are all ONE single body of energy When one of us is affected negatively, then we are all affected as it's a chain reaction. If you are going through major challenges in your life, call upon Archangel Raphael He is there to help you from within, and also to guide you out of any darkness that have been placed around you, bathing you in emerald light and bringing you back into to divine healing light. Archangel Raphael will bring you back to balance and full health in all areas of your life.

Astrological Sign: Virgo
Ruling Day: Sunday
Chakra: Third Eye, Heart
Physical Associations: Pituitary gland, Pineal Gland, Sight (inner & outer), Heart, Circulatory System
Crystals: Aventurine, Citrine, Emerald, Malachite, Yellow Calcite
Essential Oils: Carnation, Chamomile, Clove, Juniper, Lavender, Lemon, Mimosa, Neroli, Palmarosa, Pimento, Berry, Pine, Rose, Sandalwood, Spearmint, Thyme
Candle Colours: Green and blue for healing ourselves and Mother Earth. Baby Pink when healing children

Call upon Archangel Raphael to assist when:

๏ You need help to heal yourself and others
๏ You need to find a doctor, surgeon, alternative therapist or need a medical diagnosis or surgery
๏ You need to increase your levels of compassion, love and forgiveness to help heal others
๏ You are a researcher or medical scientist looking for a cure
๏ You are in pain, whether emotional or physical
๏ You are in need of help in healing deep wounds from your past experiences
๏ You need help healing and repairing a relationship

Prayer to Archangel Raphael

"Beloved Archangel Raphael, I call upon you to heal my being. My soul cries out to be healed and my

strength has gone from my body. I surrender to the Divine Creator...I surrender to God Almighty. I ask that you, beloved Raphael, heal my heart from the deepest wounds, the ones that are carved in my chest taking me away from my path in the light. Remove all darkness that has been placed around my soul, bathe me with your divine emerald light and bring back full balance to my life. I cry out for you to, send your army of healing angels my way so once again my heart and soul is restored to full divine glory. I ask in certainty that my prayer is being heard and for that I thank you in gratitude. I am ready to let go and for my healing to begin."

Archangel Chamuel

Archangel Chamuel is the Archangel of Pure Unconditional Divine Love. His name means "He who Seeks God" or "He who sees God".

He is a very loving and kind angel, the true representation of God's/Universal love. He is the master of healing all the matters of the heart.

Archangel Chamuel is well known for helping us improve and build strong foundations in relationships, allowing health and happiness to rule over them.

Archangel Chamuel always reminds us that we are never truly alone, and he ensures that in our darkest moments, when the challenges of life overwhelm us, that God is there by our side comforting us even if we don't see it.

This powerful but loving Archangel governs the path of Judgement, Justice and Severity, where retribution of karma are enacted. He is a fearless warrior, often called "The God of War". He keeps balance and order in all spiritual realms.

Astrological Sign: Aries
Ruling Day: Tuesday
Chakra: Heart
Physical Associations: Heart, Lungs, Skin, Hands, Shoulders
Crystals: Rose Quartz, Amber
Plants/Essential Oils: Angelica, Sage, Rose, Benzoin, Chamomile, Frankincense, Geranium, Hyacinth, Lavender, Mandarin, Melissa, Neroli, Violets

Candle Colours: Pink (for matters of the heart), Yellow (for uplifting, spiritual growth, fertility) and Green (for deep grounding to the energies of Mother Earth)

Call upon Archangel Chamuel to assist you when:

       You need to bring inner love to your heart you and to start healing deep from within

       You need to mend a broken heart and once again feel love for others

       You feel lonely or someone has hurt you deeply

       You need assistance to let go of pain from past relationships

       You want to fill your heart with joy and happiness

       You need help in opening your heart to finding new and true love in your life

       You are being misunderstood by others, as he can protect us from malice or slander

       World peace needs to be restored with urgency

Prayer to Archangel Chamuel

"I call upon Archangel Chamuel to be with me now. My sweet beloved Archangel of love, to your presence I come with an open heart and ask you that that you fill me with God's divine unconditional love. Let your beloved light be a sharp beam of divine love so I may release all negative stuck emotions that have stained my heart due to pain. Help me once again feel pure love for myself and for others, dissolve now all negativity in my heart that is stopping me from giving and receiving unconditional love. Bring to me once again the glow to my heart that is the mirror of my soul when touched by the divine Holy Spirit of God. I am grateful as I know in

my heart you are touching my life and heart. I thank you in advance for the blessings in my life."

Archangel Metatron

Archangel Metatron is the angel of "Ascension" and considered to be the most supreme in all of the angel's hierarchies. He has been given many names such as "King of Angels", "Chancellor of Heaven", and "Angel of the Covenant". He is a Guardian of the Tree of Life, and is the keeper of the Akashic Records, recording all of our karmic deeds in the Book of Life and reporting to the Lords and Ladies of Karma.

He is the only Archangel known to embody a human form. For this reason he has greater understanding and compassion for all of humanity and their deeper emotions. One of his missions is to help us realize and understand our true potential and limitless spiritual resources, reminding us that we were created out of Divine Unconditional Love, and it is only this form of love that makes us loving and worthy as human divine beings of light.

When Archangel Metatron is around you, he always ensures that his presence is noticed - he may come to you with a "bang" as he has quite a fiery presence! You may be witness to bright flashes of light, or he may also appear in the form of a very bright colourful aura.

Archangel Metatron acts as a pillar of Divine Light that comes down through our crown chakra, especially during periods of meditation, filling our body with pure unconditional love and divine light. He is like the bridge between worlds, cleaning and healing deeply before we access the divine spiritual realms.

Astrological Sign: Capricorn, Aries
Ruling Day: Thursday
Chakra: Crown
Physical Associations: Pineal Gland, Pituitary Gland
Crystals: Clear Quartz, Watermelon Tourmaline
Essential Oils: Lavender, Ylang Ylang, Sunflower
Candle Colours: Yellow, Gold (represents the Sun)

Call upon Archangel Metatron to assist you when:

◎   You need help changing your negative thought patterns
◎   You need to find balance in your inner self
◎   You need to clear all strands of negativity
◎   You need spiritual growth and transformation
◎   You need to release old karmic bonds
◎   You need to transmute and release stuck energies like selfishness, envy, greed or anger

Prayer to Archangel Metatron:

"Almighty Archangel Metatron, I call upon you in this moment, as I'm moving in life through troubled waters and my mind is taking over my heart, leaving me in confusion. I ask that you clear all my negative thoughts and bring spiritual clarity. I ask you humble in my heart that you clear and transmute all negative emotions, remove deep from my heart all selfishness, envy, greed, anger, ego, pride, and all negative emotions that are not from the divine or are stopping my spiritual growth and inner transformation. Once you have experienced being in human form, and you know all the emotional challenges with greater compassion, for that

I ask that you renew my body, spirit, soul and specially my mind so I live my life from my heart and not from my mind as she plays tricks on me and often guides me in the wrong direction.

Beloved Metatron I ask that you intervene before the Lords and Ladies of Karma on my behalf, cleansing and clearing my karma in all direction and time lines. If I was to have known that my actions would have impacted on my soul journey and that of others I would not have taken them, for that I ask to be forgiven. I ask that you purify me so I can better connect with God, angels and with my spirit guides.

I thank you for listening to me, and I know in my heart that you are already working on me and I am eternally grateful."

Archangel Uriel

Archangel Uriel is one of the most powerful of the Angels and his name means "The Light of God" or "God is my light". He rules over the mental plane of existence, when working under his vibration, he will be bringing you peace of mind and new helpful ideas, by removing all negative thoughts and analytic thinking.

Archangel Uriel is also one of the archangels who has been assigned to watch over Mother Earth consciousness and that of humankind. He is the Guardian of the great mysteries of life. He is one of the Seven Mighty Archangels that stand before the Throne of God, and is among the Four Mighty Archangels, Guardians of the Throne, whose task is specifically to help Humanity evolve and ascend. He is leader of the Seraphim hierarchy of angels who are Guardians of the Great Veil of Consciousness.

He is known as the Angel of Peace, the White Dove and can heal all painful memories that are embedded in the sub-conscious mind, liberating and transmuting the energy associated with them, bathing these blocked memories with his Divine Light, and therefore starting the healing process.

Astrological Sign: Taurus, Virgo, Capricorn
Ruling Day: Saturday
Chakra: Root, Heart
Physical Associations: Feet, Legs, Knees, Hips, Large intestine, Reproductive organs, Genitals, Circulatory system, Heart

Crystals: Angelite, Hematite, Obsidian, Ruby, Tiger's eye

Essential Oils: Carnation, Chamomile, Lavender, Mandarin, Melissa, Myrtle, Rose, Sandalwood

Candle Colours: Violet, indigo, white and gold; all of which are soothing colours and are associated with the higher chakras or higher realms of consciousness.

Call upon Archangel Uriel to assist you when:

☉ You need mental clarity, inner peace, or anytime you need to release painful past memories.

☉ You need help to forgive you, others, and allow yourself to let go of your blame and anger.

☉ You need to find inner peace

☉ You need to let go of inner turmoil and to release deep fears and anxieties

☉ You need stability in your life, like relationships, job or home

☉ You need to release anger and irritation

☉ You wish for peace to be bestowed upon the world, ending conflicts and suffering

☉ You need help letting go of ego and pride

☉ You need your inner strength, self-esteem, charisma and confident to be boosted

Prayer to Archangel Uriel:

"I call upon you my dear beloved Archangel Uriel and I ask you to release all the fears from my being, fill my heart with divine peace, tranquillity and pure joy. Take out the scales from my eyes that are stopping me to see clearly my divine path. May I always be a vessel of pure divine light to help others in their moments of need,

bringing them comfort in times of need. May my hands help clear the tears of those crying in despair. My words and deeds be always in truth, honour and integrity and my actions a living testimonial of God in me. I ask you to illuminate my spiritual path, so I'm able to serve others as once others served me, and so I can fulfil my life purpose and bring peace to the world. I'm ready to let go of my entire ego, pride and all that has been stopping me from growing spiritually. I thank you in advance as I know in my heart that my prayer is being answered."

About Lidia Antunes-Frederico

Lidia Frederico is a lifelong consciousness facilitator spiritual life coach, energy therapist, trance medium and author. She is widely sought out by clients and media worldwide. Originally from Portugal, she now is based in London. Lidia inherited her medium and healing abilities from a lineage of female healers and mediums on her

mother's side. Lidia has been fully aware of her gifts since childhood, which she nurtured and in due course this culminated in her developing her channeling abilities around 1993. After having practiced Karate as a child, Lidia opened her own dojo in Lisbon (Portugal) by the time she was 18, and she is now a Third Dan black belt. At this school, which is still running to this day, Lidia taught children, adults and disabled people. As a natural creative, Lidia turned her hand to being a beautician and later enjoyed a long career with government security services. Lidia is affectionately called 'the cleaner' as she expertly and thoroughly clears clients of negative influences in their energy fields. By channeling her guides, Lidia identifies all such influences in a person's life. Depending on the client, this could be anything from a person's beliefs, thought patterns, entities that have attached and need removing, or the result of those not channeling the light and much more. Whilst trance channeling, her guides pinpoint how a person's life is blocked by unwanted energies, people and situations. They proceed to move away the unwanted influences, sending them back to the light or neutralizing their influences on a person's life. She then works with each client at an energetic level for between three and six months depending on the degree of ongoing support that is necessary. The objective of Lidia's work is to get clients back on track with the life they were destined to fulfill. Lidia continues to clean and balance each client's energy field without interfering with that person until they can stand fully on their own two feet and, ensuring that unwanted influences do not return. She is an Energy and Crystal Therapist, works with chakras and auras and uses herbs for clearing and cleansing. Lidia is highly adept at soul retrieval and clearing issues from past lives, which is an area that is becoming more widely known to the greater public as a holistic healing modality. Her abilities extend to her having the ability to access the Akashic records of individuals to clear up past karma, thus enabling their life to flow once again. It is purely through her faith and belief in a higher power that Lidia has been able to evolve spiritually as she has. This has enabled her to assist those in need of her support at a profoundly deep level. Lidia's dedication to contribution and service to her family, community and planet is aligned with the Sacred Mother Energy that is urgently needed for the spiritual evolution of Humanity. Her greatest joy is in assisting people raise their spiritual frequency and, hence the planet, by helping them live a fruitful, joyous and happy life.

Also by Lidia Frederico

<u>Books</u>

"Little Treasures from Heaven"
(A guide to spiritual protection)

<u>*Subliminal Packages*</u>

Weight Loss
Brain Power
Financial Freedom
Love Yourself
Larger Breasts
Light Worker

<u>*Online Courses*</u>

The True Law of Life Course
LightWorker Foundation Course

For information on all the above products please visit:

www.lidiafrederico.com

www.lidiafredericotraininginstitute.com

We hope you have enjoyed this angelic book.
If you would like to be informed in advance of release
dates or to receive a free premier issue of Lidia
Frederico's newsletter, please contact us:

contact@lidiafrederico.com

For more information on Lidia Frederico's work,
seminars and workshops, please contact us via e-mail:

info@lidiafrederico.com